# LIVELY LEGENDS — JEWISH VALUES

## AN EARLY CHILDHOOD TEACHING GUIDE

Miriam P. Feinberg and Rena Rotenberg

With a Foreword by Saul Wachs

A.R.E. Publishing, Inc.
an imprint of Behrman House, Inc.
Springfield, New Jersey

Published by:
A.R.E. Publishing, Inc.
an imprint of Behrman House, Inc.
Springfield, New Jersey
www.behrmanhouse.com

Library of Congress Catalog Card Number 93-70474
ISBN 10: 0-86705-030-6
ISBN 13: 978-0-86705-030-1

© A.R.E. Publishing, Inc. 1993

Printed in the United States of America

All rights reserved. No part of this book may be reproduced
in any form or by any means without permission in writing
from the publisher.

## CONTENTS

Acknowledgements ..................................................................................v
Foreword ..............................................................................................vii
Introduction ..........................................................................................ix

*The Value of Extending Hospitality*
   1   Elijah the Prophet ..................................................................1
   2   What's Missing? ....................................................................11

*The Value of Treating Animals Kindly*
   3   The Stolen Donkey ...............................................................25
   4   The Bell of Justice ................................................................37

*The Value of Caring for Nature*
   5   Honi Ha-Meagel Sleeps for Seventy Years ...........................47
   6   The Best Blessing .................................................................59
   7   King Solomon and the Bee ...................................................69

*The Value of Hard Work*
   8   Nicanor's Door .....................................................................79

*The Value of Sharing With the Poor*
   9   Three Loaves ........................................................................95
  10   The Treasure ......................................................................111

*The Value of Honesty*
  11   Honest Scales .....................................................................127
  12   Little Becomes Much .........................................................139
  13   The Precious Jewel ............................................................157

*The Value of Learning*
  14   An Old Young Student .......................................................169
  15   The Good Teacher ..............................................................185

*The Value of Caring for Loved Ones*
  16   Two Brothers .....................................................................193
  17   Visiting a Sick Friend ........................................................207

*Bibliography* .....................................................................................221

# ACKNOWLEDGEMENTS

This book could not have been written and published without the assistance, encouragement, and enthusiasm of colleagues and friends.

We extend heartfelt thanks to:

Dr. Saul Wachs who inspired us with the idea for this work, saw its value, and believed in our abilities to see the project through to completion.

Ofra Reisman and Nehama Nir Yaniv who served as role models and teachers to us through their dedication to their work.

The teachers who enthusiastically field tested our work and offered suggestions. Lynette Berman and Liz Novick of Baltimore Hebrew Congregation Preschool and Day School respectively; Marlene Zytcer and Hattie Katkow of Bet Yeladim Nursery and Day Care Center; Bonnie Walker, Susan Albert, and Rachel Meisels of Chizuk Amuno Early Childhood Education Center; and Ann Goldberg of Gan Yeladim Child Care Center, all of Baltimore; Dina Korman of the Hebrew Day Institute of Rockville, Maryland; Sharon Mervis and Jackie Portnoy of Washington Hebrew Congregation Nursery School and Kindergarten in Potomac, Maryland.

Our wonderfully insightful and creative editors, Rabbi Raymond A. Zwerin and Audrey Friedman Marcus of A.R.E. Publishing, who recognized the importance of this work and very skillfully directed its progress.

In the process of writing this book, we always considered the children for whom it was created. Who could better exemplify the next generation than our own grandchildren, Avraham Rotenberg, Chaim Elimelech Rotenberg, Chaim Simcha Rotenberg, Tzvi Aharon Rotenberg, and Matan Moshe Feinberg, who bring us joy and hope for the future?

# FOREWORD

A high quality early childhood Jewish education is significant in nurturing Jewish identity; the rich educative experiences gained therein can serve as a solid foundation for a lifetime of Jewish learning and Jewish living.

While the field is blessed with committed educators of vision and energy, in short supply are learning materials that are content rich *and* educationally sophisticated. How fortunate then that two leading Jewish early childhood educators have collaborated again to bring us a major resource for teaching Jewish values and for creating Jewish experiences.

*Aggadah* — the story, the legend, the parable — has the power to move us and to teach us. We love to hear stories, we remember stories, we tell stories. But there is more to *aggadah* than mere enjoyment, or play, or esthetics. Our Rabbis thought it to be a means of profound understanding: "If you wish to get to know the One by whose word the world came into being — study the *Aggadah*" (*Sifrei Devarim* 49).

Yes, it is through stories that we come to understand and appreciate the spiritual dimensions of life. Through *aggadot*, our Rabbis taught us what they believed about God and people and life. While *halachah*, Jewish law, created norms that unified the Jewish community, in the realm of *aggadah* each person was and is free to imagine and to speculate, to instruct and to wonder. *Aggadah* illustrates the values and concepts — the Jewish terminology upon which Rabbinic theology is based. Through such accounts we learn about and come to appreciate *Kiddush Hashem* (behavior that sanctifies God's name) and *Hillul Hashem* (behavior that desecrates God's name), Talmud Torah (the study of Torah), *Tzedakah*, *Kibbud Av V'Em* (honoring of father and mother), *Chesed* (loving-kindness), *Gevurah* (courage), *Derech Eretz* (good manners and practical wisdom), *Tza'ar Ba'alei Chayim* (sensitivity to the pain suffered by living creatures), *Ahavat Yisrael* (love of Jews), and *Ahavat Hab'riyot* (love of human beings).

*Aggadot* depict real struggles faced by real people in the past; dressed in modern garb, the same struggles are still with us today. They also depict how great and simple people alike tried to resolve their difficulties and the results of their efforts. Thus, *aggadot* functioned and can still function as tools for gaining perspective, insight, and wisdom.

I have had some difficulties with the standard practice of teaching the weekly Torah portion to the very young. I have wondered about the possible impact of such stories as the Flood, the destruction of Sodom, the near sacrifice of Isaac, and the destruction of Korah upon young and tender minds. But I have no such concerns about the collection of *aggadot* found in this volume. When we study *aggadah*, we are free to stress that these are teaching stories and not necessarily the reportage of actual events. Here we are free to allow the widest possible latitude of interpretation among the pupils, without any concern that we may be deviating from the strictures of tradition.

Miriam Feinberg and Rena Rotenberg have rendered a signal service to parents and teachers everywhere by selecting gems from our *aggadic* literature and presenting them in language that is age appropriate, together with a rich assortment of questions, as well as creative follow-up activities for home and school. This book makes it possible for young children everywhere to enjoy a few of the treasures of Rabbinic literature and folklore, and to learn about the beliefs, ideas, and values which are at the core of our Jewish heritage.

I hope that this book proves to be the first of many such collections of *aggadot* to enrich the resources of Jewish early childhood education while, at the same time, affording opportunities for intergenerational learning — at home and in the school.

Dr. Saul P. Wachs<br>
Rosaline B. Feinstein Professor of Education<br>
Gratz College

# INTRODUCTION

## *Origin of the Project*

During a Shabbat dinner in Jerusalem, Dr. Saul Wachs, Rosaline B. Feinstein Professor of Education at Gratz College, impressed upon us the importance of legends in the process of transmitting Jewish experiences and spirituality. It was at his urging that we began this book.

When Ofra Reisman and Nehama Nir Yaniv, under the auspices of the World Zionist Organization Early Childhood Department, published their versions of a variety of Jewish legends, we knew that we were on the right track — that such a book for English speaking early childhood educators was needed in order to fill an obvious gap in Jewish curriculum materials.

By and large, early childhood Jewish educators have not been presenting such tales to their young students. Often, they do not know where to find relevant, engaging stories. Further, they feel uncomfortable in presenting material that may not be appropriate in language or content for their three to seven-year-old students. In addition, teachers have expressed a desire to identify methods and materials for teaching values to young children within a Jewish framework. We are convinced that the appropriate way to do this is through the telling of legends such as are contained in this book.

## *Why Tell Jewish Legends to Young Children*

Storytelling is an ancient, long-lived art which transmits the hopes and fears, prayers and aspirations, history and values of a people. For countless centuries, stories have been passed from one generation to another as a way of preserving a people's past while imprinting its identity on the present. Not only the story, but the process of storytelling also has a life of its own. The storyteller finds satisfaction in creating a mental image, and the listener, intrigued by the direct and personal sharing of the teller, delights in visiting the "world" portrayed.

Young children especially love to hear stories; they are an unfailingly appreciative and admiring audience. Since it is evident that children not only enjoy the medium, but are capable of tremendous learning by way of it, then why not present Jewish stories to our children? The legends collected in this book are not only engaging and age appropriate, they are also value laden and peopled by individuals who lived by these values. By reading and rereading these legends aloud, the children will become familiar with the names and character traits of

Jewish people from ages past. They will gain familiarity with stories that Jews have loved to tell for ages, thus linking this youngest group of Jews to their people through a common literature.

## *Selecting Stories*

As alluded to above, of the countless Jewish legends extant, most are simply not appropriate for young children either because of theme or the concepts portrayed. After an exhaustive search, we selected this sampling of stories with themes, characters, and plots which we felt were suitable. Nonetheless, most of these stories required considerable reworking before they were ready for reading to our audience. We have not hesitated to "massage" plot, characterization, language, and concepts throughout. Also, it does not take a very long look at Jewish folk literature to notice that women play a minuscule part in such tales. So, to create a balance, we unabashedly wrote women into some of our selections.

There are, of course, other legends that might be adapted for younger children. To that end, a number of collections of such legends are described in the Bibliography at the end of this book.

## *About This Book*

### The Format

In our book *Torah Talk: An Early Childhood Teaching Guide*, we responded to a need on the part of early childhood teachers for a guide by which to present Bible stories. Because the format of that book has been successful, we are using the same format in *Lively Legends — Jewish Values: An Early Childhood Teaching Guide*.

### Contents and Structure

The stories are ordered according to Jewish values. These values are especially significant and fitting for young children. They are: the value of extending hospitality, the value of treating animals kindly, the value of caring for nature, the value of hard work, the value of sharing with the poor, the value of honesty, the value of learning, and the value of caring for loved ones.

Each chapter is structured according to the following divisions:

### Before Telling the Story

This section is as useful as it is unusual. Learning, much like any physical activity, benefits from a preliminary "warm up," so to speak. It is important that the listener come to the story in the right frame of reference. Terminology should be understood before it is confronted in the story; the stage for what is about to be heard should be set. This section is intended to do all of the above — establishing continuity with events past and setting the tone for events to come.

### Telling the Story

This section contains the story itself, adapted for the early childhood level. All of the stories are set in larger type so that they may be read more easily. Following each story are questions to discuss with the children. These questions are based strictly on information in the story.

### Themes in the Story

Here you will find an outline of themes present in the story just told, as well as discussion questions for each theme under the heading "Bringing the Story Closer." The inclusion of the themes will give a focus for the teacher or parent when discussing the story with the children. The questions in this section are intended to bring the story closer to the personal day-to-day life of the young listener.

### Creative Follow-up

In every chapter there are many follow-up activities. These include a wide variety of exercises which are categorized under such headings as: Retelling the Story, Role Play, Music, Building/Creating, Game Time, Experience Chart, etc. Each of these activities is designated for three and four-year-olds, or for five and six-year-olds. Under each you will find goals (either for both similar activities or for each activity under a specific age group), a description of the activity, the materials needed, and the procedure to follow.

### Taking the Story Home

At the conclusion of the Creative Follow-up is a home component section which includes activities on the story for parents and children. It is recommended that the teacher send home a letter at the beginning of the year outlining the curriculum and informing parents of the home component which accompanies the stories. Then, as often as possible, send home a synopsis of a story, along with a listing of suggested activities for parent or parents to do with their child.

## Teaching Recommendations

### When To Tell Legends

In considering when to include legends in your curriculum, first examine the schedule of the day. Set aside a time for reading and/or telling the story when the children are most likely to feel comfortable and prepared to sit quietly and listen. A good time might be right after a snack.

You might choose to tell (or read) a particular legend from the collection in this book because it deals with a theme that connects with a recent classroom event. For example, if an item was lost and then returned to its owner, "The Precious Jewel" merits telling. Caring for pets in the classroom may provide the impetus for sharing "The Stolen Donkey." Sometimes, a story may be chosen because the theme forms the basis of a particular project or unit. For example, it would be appropriate to introduce "Nicanor's Door" when focusing on Israel or in taking pride in one's work. Two of the legends included in this book deal with Shabbat. These could be most suitable for telling at the weekly pre-Shabbat party. In the event that a pre-Shabbat party guest is present, you might like to let him or her tell (or read) the story.

Sometimes you will want to choose a story simply because it is fun to listen to and to participate in. Some of these stories may become favorites which the children want to hear again and again, each time noticing a new aspect of the plot or character development.

### How To Tell the Stories

A story may, of course, be read to children, but telling it without using the book provides a more intimate and involving sharing experience. To tell the story without referring to the text, read it aloud to yourself. Then, to become thoroughly familiar with it, read it over a second and third time. (If necessary, prepare index cards noting the major events of the story. The cards can rest on your lap during the storytelling.)

Gather the children close to you so that you can have eye contact with them as you engage them in what will be a special experience. Be sure they are sitting in a comfortable place and that they have a clear and unobstructed view of the storyteller.

As you tell the story, be prepared to ask and respond to the children's questions and interpretations. However, if questions seem to be disrupting the continuity and flow of the story, suggest that children wait to ask them until the story is finished.

Good questions asked by the teacher can reinforce an idea, challenge a child to think through a particular issue, and enhance the level of understanding. Many challenging questions on the facts of the stories and on their themes are included herein.

## *Reinforcement Opportunities*

You will find frequent mention throughout this book of opening circle, free choice activities, final circle, and pre-Shabbat party. These terms are clarified below. All of these occasions provide an opportunity to integrate Bible stories into other segments of the daily schedule. When introduced at these additional times, the material in this book is reinforced and further internalized. Finally, reference is often made to the use of experience charts and illustrations. These are also described below.

### Opening Circle

Opening circle helps the children and teacher to begin the school day. During this time, all of the children sit together in a circle on the floor (or on chairs if preferred). In the fortunate situation that there are two competent and trained adults in the classroom, the group can be divided in half and each adult can lead a small circle. (Arrange the two circles as far as possible from each other.)

Teachers generally use circle time for taking attendance, providing the children with the opportunity to share experiences with each other, and informing the children of the plans for the day. Other suggestions for using circle time to good advantage are: saying daily prayers; teaching (or reviewing) a song; joining in a finger play or reciting a poem; and discussing the calendar, the weather, and the free choice activity centers in the classroom. This time can also be used to review biblical material and/or to inform children about the new story to be introduced during class that day.

### Free Choice Activities

Some experienced teachers may feel comfortable providing as many as eight activity centers simultaneously. However, most teachers offer fewer than eight, and four is an acceptable number. The centers can be changed so that in the period of a month, many choices have been offered. Encourage children to use the activity centers to develop creative play while interacting with their peers.

### Final Circle

Many teachers find it useful to bring children together for a final circle at the end of the school day. Once again, this can be accomplished by arranging the children either in a single large circle or in two small circles. Some teachers prefer to read a story at this time; others use the time for reviewing the events of the day in a relaxed, happy manner. In the latter instance, all of the children should be given an opportunity to speak during the final circle time. Encourage the children to talk about the stories and the Creative Follow-up activities in which they participated.

**Experience Charts**

As a follow-up to the stories, the use of experience charts is an effective way to find out what the children have learned. Such charts also provide an opportunity for children to teach each other by sharing information. An experience chart should be viewed as an extension of a classroom discussion. A description of how to make and use experience charts follows.

*Materials*
   large pieces of newsprint (lined or unlined)
   an easel on which to attach the newsprint (or masking tape with which to attach the newsprint to a wall or chalkboard)
   dark felt marker or crayon

*Procedure*
1. Following a discussion, ask the children to provide additional ideas on the topic discussed.
2. Write those ideas (use sentences or single words) on the paper. If the children are too young to read, use pictures instead of, or in addition to, words. The experience chart should be no longer than a single page. The print should be clear, large, dark, and consistent, starting at the top and proceeding to the bottom of the page.
3. When the exercise is completed, review the chart with the children, asking them to "read" its contents.

**Pictures To Accompany Stories**

While illustrations have not been included in this book, we recommend creating pictures for use with the stories. The children can create pictures based upon their mental images. Or, you may wish to create the pictures for them, either as classroom decorations or flannel board and bulletin board displays. The pictures should be integrated into the retelling of the stories so that they provide a vehicle for the children to share and enhance their mental images.

## *Conclusion*

The inclusion of Jewish legends in the early childhood classroom on a regular and frequent basis offers opportunities for introducing young children to Jewish values and to Jewish folk heroes and heroines. It establishes the foundation for a lifelong appreciation of such Jewish personalities as Hillel, Honi Ha-Meagel, Rabbi Shimon Ben Shetach, and Elijah the Prophet, among others.

It is our hope that the telling of legends such as these will become part of the curriculum of every Jewish early childhood classroom. We further hope that by relating such legends and by reinforcing their message through activities that complement them, the richness of our folklore and the nobility of our values will become an integral part of the Jewish life-force of our youngest learners.

# CHAPTER 1
# *Elijah the Prophet*

## BEFORE TELLING THE STORY

Before reading the story, talk with the children about hospitality and what it means to be hospitable.

Be sure to point out that in this story, there are two kinds of guests — one who had been previously invited and the other who invited himself. Both were treated with dignity and care.

Read other stories on the subject, such as "Abraham Welcomes Guests" in *Torah Talk* by Yona Chubara, Miriam P. Feinberg, and Rena Rotenberg, and *Just Enough Room* by Miriam P. Feinberg. Discuss the rewards of extending hospitality to others.

## TELLING THE STORY

Elijah the Prophet was very curious about how the people in a certain town behaved. He decided to dress up like a beggar and wander through the streets. He walked and walked. He wandered from street to street, from store to store, and from synagogue to synagogue, watching how the people of that town treated each other.

One day he noticed a tiny house. "My goodness, this place really needs repairs!" he thought. "A new roof, painted shutters, and a better gate would help! But look at these beautiful flowers in the little front yard."

He was tired and hungry from walking so much, and the flowers were so pretty and inviting that Elijah decided to stop at this house to rest.

"Knock, knock," he rapped. And in a short while, a poor man and his wife came to the door.

"Oh, please come in," said the couple, smiling. Noticing how tired Elijah looked, they asked, "Would you like something to drink?" And noticing how hungry he was, they suggested, "Even though we don't have much dinner to offer, we'd like you to eat with us. Having a guest makes a meal seem more special." And the three of them sat down to share the tiny meal.

After eating, Elijah said, "Because you have been so kind, I will grant you three wishes. Tell me three things that you want and I will give them to you."

The husband sat quietly and thought to himself, "I wonder if this guest can really grant me three wishes. There does seem to be something unusual about him. Let me see . . . what should I wish for?"

After a few quiet moments, he explained, "This tiny house is falling apart! And I don't have enough room for my books. I wish I could have a house as large as . . . a . . . a . . . palace!"

At that, Elijah whistled and — poof — a beautiful mansion stood where the tiny house had been.

The wife looked down at her ragged clothes. She took off her old worn apron and shook her head. "Look at us! We look so plain and poor in this beautiful house! We need gorgeous clothes and sparkly jewelry!"

Then Elijah whistled a second time and — poof — in an instant the couple was dressed in velvet and satin. The wife wore jewelry of diamonds, pearls, and emeralds.

Suddenly the couple shouted together, "Gold, gold, we need gold!"

Again Elijah whistled and — poof — sacks of gold appeared. And with that, Elijah disappeared.

Many years passed. Elijah was curious about the couple. So he decided to dress up like a beggar again and go back to the place where they lived.

When he came to their big fancy house, he saw heavy shutters on the windows and high fences all around the house. There was a lot of land, but no flowers, no trees, and no grass.

"Go away!" the servants yelled at Elijah. "Beggars aren't allowed here!"

"I want to see the people who own this house," Elijah explained.

The servants laughed at Elijah and brought their dogs to the gate to scare him away.

"What's all this noise!" shouted the owner of the house. "Go away beggar, or we'll chase you away," he yelled, not recognizing Elijah.

"How sad and disappointing," Elijah thought to himself. Then he whistled once, and — poof — the gold disappeared.

He whistled again and — poof — the beautiful clothes and jewels disappeared.

Then he whistled a third time and — poof — the tiny, run-down house stood where the beautiful mansion had been before.

At that moment, the couple knew how selfish they had become. And, they also realized that they would be much, much happier in their tiny, old house than they had ever been in their fancy palace. "Now we're really rich!" they said to each other as they smiled and hugged.

**Questions on The Story**
1. Why did Elijah visit the town?
2. How did Elijah know that a poor family lived in the tiny house?
3. What did he learn about the couple when he visited them?
4. How did the couple change when they were given more things?
5. How did Elijah feel about them when they changed their behavior?
6. Did you like the couple better when they had more things or fewer? Why?
7. If you had three wishes, what would you wish for?

## THEMES IN THE STORY

### *The importance of extending hospitality*
The couple invited Elijah to have dinner with them, and to share their small meal.

*Bringing the theme closer*
- How does a welcomed guest feel?
- How do you think Elijah felt when the couple shared their dinner with him?
- Have you ever shared something with a friend? What was it?

### *The importance of sharing with those in need*
The couple saw Elijah as a poor man who came to them in need. Without questioning him, they shared their meager meal with him.

*Bringing the theme closer*
- Did you ever share something with someone you never met? What was it?
- What things can you share with others?

# CREATIVE FOLLOW-UP

## *Retelling the Story*

### Goals
To help the children sequence the events of the story.
To give them an understanding of the story's events.

### FILL IN THE BLANKS (3 AND 4-YEAR-OLDS)

#### Description of Activity
Children help to retell the story in their own words.

#### Materials
none

#### Procedure
1. Gather the children together in a circle.
2. Begin retelling the story.
3. Pause when you reach the point where Elijah speaks with the couple.
4. Encourage each of the children to take a turn filling in with his/her own words what Elijah and the couple said to each other during their meal together. For example, they might talk about the things they were doing before they met, what they plan to do after they finish their meal, etc.
5. Continue this activity until every child has had a turn or until interest wanes.

### DRAW AND SHOW (5 AND 6-YEAR-OLDS)

#### Description of Activity
The children are encouraged to draw pictures of the couple's simple house and of their palace, of their simple clothing and of their fancy outfits.

#### Materials
drawing paper
felt markers
crayons

## Procedure

1. Gather 5 or 6 children together to discuss the story.
2. Invite each child to draw four pictures; one picture showing the couple's house before they were granted their wish, another picture showing their palace, a third picture showing the couple in the clothes which they wore before they were granted their wish, and the fourth picture showing them in their fancy clothing when they lived in their palace.
3. Gather other groups of children together and repeat the activity.
4. When all of the children have had the opportunity to complete their pictures, form a circle.
5. Invite the children to take turns talking about their pictures.
6. Upon completion of this activity, display all of the pictures on a bulletin board. Label them: The Couple's Simple House, The Couple's Palace, The Couple's Simple Clothing, The Couple's Fancy Clothing.

## *Make a Story*

### Goals
To encourage the children to think creatively.

### GOING TO THE TOWN (3 AND 4-YEAR-OLDS)

### Description of Activity
The children make up stories about Elijah and his trip to the town.

### Materials
tape recorder

## Procedure

1. Gather a small group of children together and ask them to explain why Elijah went to the town. Other questions to ask:
   What did Elijah do in the town once he arrived there?
   How did Elijah get to the town?
   What did Elijah carry with him to the town?
2. Each child is given a turn to talk into a tape recorder on this topic. Some children may need assistance from the teacher.
3. After each child has had a turn, the class can listen to the tape.

## GOING TO THE TOWN (5 AND 6-YEAR-OLDS)

### Description of the Activity
The children write stories about Elijah.

### Materials
drawing paper
felt markers
staplers

### Procedure
1. Gather a group of children together. Provide paper and felt markers, and encourage each of them to dictate a story about Elijah and his reasons for going to the town.
2. Following the dictation, encourage the children to draw pictures on their papers depicting Elijah and his journey to the town.
3. The children may prepare as many illustrated stories as they wish. If they prepare several, they may choose to combine them into a book by stapling them together.
4. When all of the children have completed the project, each child can "read" his/her story to the others at circle time. You might decide to introduce the "reading" of the stories at several circle times in order to give each child an appropriate amount of time to share.

## Food Experiences

### SIMPLY A ROYAL TREAT (3 AND 4-YEAR-OLDS)

**Description of Activity**
The children learn to make plain food fancy.

**Materials**
lowfat yogurt or cottage cheese (enough for each child)
toppings: fresh sliced fruit (pineapple, banana, strawberries, orange sections), raisins, sprinkles, chocolate chips
bowls (one for each child and one for each of the food items above)
spoons (one for each child and one for each of the food items above)

**Procedure**
1. After telling the story, tell the children that each of them will have an opportunity to make a special treat to be eaten at snack time.
2. Gather together a small group of children. Begin by directing them to wash their hands with soap and water.
3. Bring the children to a table with all of the materials listed above within easy reach.
4. Introduce a discussion of the foods that can be put on top of plain yogurt or cottage cheese to make it more interesting, unusual, and/or tasty.
5. Encourage the children to place yogurt, cottage cheese, and toppings into their bowls as they wish.
6. After the food creations have been made, mark each bowl with the name of the creator, then refrigerate the bowls.
7. Repeat this prcedure with other small groups of children until all have had an opportunity to create their own snacks.
8. At snack time, bring out the refrigerated snacks. Recite the appropriate blessing before eating them:

*Baruch Atah Adonai Eloheynu Melech Ha-olam Shehakol Neh'yeh Bidvaro.*

Blessed are You, Eternal our God, Ruler of the universe, by Whose word all things come into being.

## HATS OFF TO ELIJAH (5 and 6-YEAR-OLDS)

**Description of Activity**
The children make and decorate hats using newspaper and tape.

**Materials**
newspaper
masking tape
tupperware bowl about the size of a child's head
collage materials (pieces of felt, pieces of ribbon, cotton balls, sparkles, etc.)
a mixture of half glue and half water

**Procedure**
1. Gather together a small group of children during free choice activity time.
2. Place three sheets of newspaper (criss-crossed in three directions) on the first child's head. If a child objects to the newspaper being placed on his/her head, substitute a tupperware bowl.
3. Another child or adult then holds the newspaper on the crown of the child's head as the teacher wraps masking tape around the forehead, both sides, and the back of the head. Make sure the tape is snug.
4. Lift the newspaper from the head or the bowl and decorate in any way desired. The rim of the newspaper may be rolled up and taped if desired.
5. Explain that the fancier the hat, the more it indicates the wealth of the individual.
6. Cover the completed hat with a mixture of half glue and half water.
7. Allow the hat to dry until very hard.

Front          Back

8. Upon completion of this activity by the first group, invite other small groups of children to participate until all have had an opportunity to make a hat.
9. After all the children have created at least one hat, encourage them to model and/or display their creations, and to describe them at circle time.

## TAKING THE STORY HOME

1. **Button People**
Suggest that family members recreate the story by making and using button people as follows:

   **Materials**
   large buttons
   construction paper of various colors
   glue sticks or white glue
   felt markers or crayons

   **Procedure**
   1. After telling the story, gather the materials together, making them easily accessible.
   2. On a table, lay out an assortment of buttons, glue, and drawing implements.
   3. Family members can use the materials to make pictures of people in the story.
   4. As the button people are being created, talk about them and which people in the story they represent.

2. **Hospitality**
Families can discuss situations in which it is appropriate to extend hospitality. For instance:
   a. Welcoming guests who visit without having previously been invited.
   b. Inviting a guest for Shabbat dinner.
   c. Inviting guests to a family gathering.

3. **Wishing**
During a family "talk-time," each family member can write down or dictate three wishes — one for him/herself, one for the benefit of the family, and one to benefit the Jewish people. Then each family member in turn can share his or her wishes with the others.

## CHAPTER 2
# *What's Missing?*

## BEFORE TELLING THE STORY

Before telling the story below, initiate a discussion on ways that friends teach each other, and things that they learn. Ask: Have you ever learned something from a friend? Do you think you ever taught a friend something new? What was it?

Inform the children that you will tell them a story about two friends who learned some things from each other.

## TELLING THE STORY

Rabbi Judah HaNasi lived in Israel, in the town of Bet She'arim. One of his friends was Emperor Antonius, who was the ruler in Israel.

One Saturday, Emperor Antonius thought, "I haven't seen Rabbi Judah HaNasi in a long time. I think I'll visit him and see how he and his family are doing." So the Emperor went to Rabbi Judah's house and knocked on the door.

"What a wonderful surprise and an honor!" said Rabbi Judah, smiling and shaking his friend's hand. "Come in, Emperor, and join me and my family for Shabbat afternoon dinner."

Rabbi Judah brought Emperor Antonius into the dining room where the family was already at the table. They were eating *challah*, fruit, and cold meat, and drinking wine."

"We're having a cold meal now because on Shabbat we don't cook food. Please sit down and join us," suggested Rabbi Judah.

"What a marvelous invitation," answered the Emperor, as he took a seat next to his friend.

Antonius tasted one of the foods on his plate. He liked it, so he tasted another food. That one tasted even better. Pretty soon, he ate everything on his plate and asked for more.

Then Rabbi Judah and his family sang some Shabbat songs. "Sing some *z'mirot* with us," suggested Rabbi Judah. And the Emperor hummed along with the melody. He liked the way the songs sounded.

Between the eating and the singing, Rabbi Judah and his family talked. Even the conversation seemed special to Emperor Antonius. What a time he was having!

As he was leaving he told the family, "The meal was absolutely delicious! I've never tasted such good food."

"I'm so glad that you enjoyed it," said Rabbi Judah. "You must come back and have another meal with us some time soon."

"Yes, yes, I certainly will," answered Emperor Antonius.

Sure enough, several days later, Rabbi Judah heard a rap at his door. "Well, hello, Emperor," said the Rabbi as he invited his friend in.

"The other day, you invited me to come back soon for a meal with you, so here I am," explained the Emperor.

"Wonderful, wonderful!" exclaimed Rabbi Judah. "You're just in time for dinner. And today, the food will be warm because it is not Shabbat and we can cook." The men sat down at the dinner table with the rest of the family and began to eat the steaming hot food.

The Emperor tasted one thing, then another, then another, and still another. After he had tasted everything, he said, "Something is different. This food is good, but not as tasty as the last meal. Do you think that the cook might have forgotten to add a certain spice?"

"You're right, Emperor," explained Rabbi Judah. "There is a missing spice."

"Then tell me what it is, Rabbi, and I will order it from the kitchen in the palace. Whatever that spice is and wherever it is grown, I will get it for you!"

"Oh, no," explained the Rabbi." The spice cannot be found today in any kitchen, not even in the kitchen of a palace. And you can't buy it anywhere. The spice can only be found in food that is served on Shabbat. Shabbat is a very, very special day, and everything that is served on that day tastes special."

"Shabbat is certainly a wonderful spice," said the Emperor, "and today was a wonderful day. I've learned something new and important today."

**Questions on the Story**
1. Why did Rabbi Judah invite his friend for Shabbat dinner?
2. What kinds of special Shabbat foods do you think were served at that dinner?

3. Why was the food served cold?
4. Why didn't the food taste as good when it wasn't Shabbat?
5. Have you ever heard of an emperor? What do you think an emperor is?
6. Do you know the name of an emperor or a king?

## THEMES IN THE STORY

### Hospitality
Rabbi Judah HaNasi exemplified hospitality by inviting the emperor to have dinner with him and his family.

*Bringing the Theme Closer*
- What do you do when a guest comes to your house?
- Do you offer food to your guest? What kind of food?

### Making Shabbat Special
Emperor Antonius could tell that the meal served on Shabbat was more special than a meal served on any other day of the week. Rabbi Judah and his family had done something to make Shabbat a special day.

*Bringing the Theme Closer*
- What makes Shabbat different from any other day of the week?
- Does Shabbat food taste different from weekday food? Why or why not?
- Do you know of any foods that people like to eat on Shabbat? What are they?

### The Importance of Enhancing Shabbat
Rabbi Judah and his family made Shabbat as beautiful and special as they could. They prepared special foods, sang Shabbat songs, and invited guests to share their meal with them.

*Bringing the Theme Closer*
- In what ways did Rabbi Judah and his family make Shabbat beautiful and special?
- What can you do to make Shabbat special in your house? (Suggest such things as eating in the dining room instead of the kitchen, using special dishes that are different from the everyday ones, serving special foods, singing Shabbat songs, wearing special clothes, etc.)
- Which of these things have you done at your house or at someone else's house?

# CREATIVE FOLLOW-UP

## *Retelling the Story*

### Goals
To reinforce information acquired during the telling of the story.
To help the children sequence the story events.
To create awareness of the perspective of others.

### ROLE PLAYING (3 AND 4-YEAR-OLDS)

**Description of Activity**
The children role play the story.

**Materials**
a large box
fancy clothing:
  a crown, jewelry, and a robe for the emperor
  a fancy *kipah*, and a robe for the Rabbi
  an apron for Rabbi Judah's wife
  scarves and a variety of *kipot* for Rabbi Judah's children
  empty food containers
  plastic play food

**Procedure**
1. Gather the children together in a semi-circle.
2. Assign roles and costumes to some of the children.
3. Begin telling the story. As each character comes into the story, the appropriate child (or children) acts out his/her part for the audience (the rest of the class).
4. This activity can be repeated, giving the children opportunities to switch roles and to be both actors and audience.

### WHAT'S FOR DINNER? (5 AND 6-YEAR-OLDS)

**Description of Activity**
The class prepares a menu for a Shabbat meal.

**Materials**
   newsprint paper
   felt markers
   tacks

**Procedure**
1. During free choice activity time, gather 4 or 5 children together.
2. Discuss with them what they think was on Rabbi Judah's Shabbat menu.
3. If the children are not yet able to write, record their responses on paper. If they are able, have them write the responses themselves.
4. Repeat with other groups of children until everyone in the class has completed the project.
5. When all of the children have completed the project, gather the class together in a circle and begin retelling the story.
6. When you reach the discussion of the meal in the story, invite the children to share information on their menus with each other.
7. Following this activity, display all of the menus on the bulletin board under the title "Rabbi Judah's Shabbat Meal."

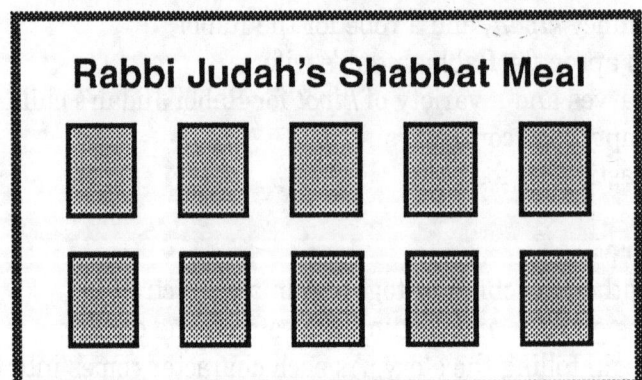

## *Preparing Shabbat Foods*

**Goals**
   To help the children experience the fun of preparing for Shabbat.
   To give them the opportunity to participate in preparing and enjoying a pre-Shabbat program.
   To provide the children with opportunities for learning about safety and health when preparing food.

## MAKING DINNER (3 AND 4-YEAR-OLDS)

### Description of Activity

*Vegetarian Liver*
(Rena Rotenberg's family recipe)

It is traditional in some homes to serve chopped liver at the Shabbat lunch meals. The following recipe is for vegetarian liver that tastes like the real thing, but does not contain the fat and cholesterol.

### Ingredients
3 eggs
1 10 oz. package of frozen lima beans
3 onions
1 tablespoon vegetable oil
1 package plain crackers

### Supplies
1 saucepan
1 frying pan
a food processor
1 wooden spoon
1 large bowl

### Procedure
1. Cook the eggs until they are hardboiled.
2. Cook the lima beans according to the directions on the package.
3. Slice the onions and saute them in the oil until they are golden brown.
4. Place the eggs, beans, and onions in the food processor and combine.
5. Add salt and pepper to taste.
6. Spread on crackers and eat.

*Challah*
(See recipe on page 102.)

## Vegetarian Chicken Soup
(Miriam Feinberg's family recipe)

**Ingredients**
- 1 gallon of water
- 6-8 cubes of pareve chicken soup mix
- 8-12 carrots
- 8-12 stalks celery
- 2-4 onions
- salt
- pepper

**Supplies**
- 1 large pot
- 1 large spoon
- 1 soup ladle
- vegetable peelers
- knives
- cutting boards
- cups
- spoons
- (provide a sufficient number of peelers, knives, cutting boards, cups, and spoons to enable all children to participate actively)

**Procedure**
1. Pour the water into the pot. Place the pot on a burner.
2. Bring the water in the pot to a boil.
3. Add the soup cubes to the boiling water and stir.
4. Wash, peel, and cut up the vegetables and add them to the mixture.
5. Cook until the vegetables are tender (15-20 minutes).
6. Taste the soup and add salt and pepper if needed.
7. Serve the soup in cups.

## Kugel

**Ingredients**
- 1 box of kugel mix

**Supplies**
   1 mixing bowl
   1 mixing spoon

**Procedure**
1. Follow cooking instructions on the box.
2. These recipes can be made on as many Thursdays and Fridays as necessary until each has been tried and served at a pre-Shabbat party.

## MAKING DINNER (5 AND 6-year-olds)

**Description of Activity**
   Using family recipes contributed by the children, prepare food for the weekly pre-Shabbat party.

**Materials**
   recipes from home
   construction paper
   felt markers

**Procedure**
1. Encourage each of the children to bring in a recipe suitable for serving at a Shabbat meal.
2. Send a note to the parents explaining the request. Encourage them also to send commentary about their contributions (source of the recipe, length of time it has been in their family, etc.). In schools which observe dietary laws, *kashrut* guidelines should be clearly explained.
3. Make an effort to try one or two of the recipes at each weekly pre-Shabbat party during the year.
4. With the help of parent volunteers, copy the recipes into a class cookbook.
5. Photocopy the book so that each child may be provided with a copy.

## *Smells, Tastes, and Appearances*

**Goals**
   To help the children develop classification skills through the use of herbs.
   To learn to associate smells with taste and appearance.
   To learn to use herbs to enhance and change of taste of foods.

### NAME THAT HERB (3 and 4-year-olds)

**Description of Activity**
　　The children are given opportunities to become familiar with a variety of herbs.

**Materials**
　　a variety of herbs (parsley, basil, oregano, thyme, dill, marjoram, cumin, cardamon, etc.)
　　a variety of herb seeds to match the herbs mentioned above
　　several small bowls
　　salad ingredients (lettuce, tomatoes, cucumber, green pepper, other fresh vegetables, etc.)
　　a bag of potting soil (enough to permit each child to fill a 4 oz. paper cup halfway)

**Procedure**
1. Gather a small group of children together.
2. Place the herbs in the bowls and arrange them on a table so that they are easily accessible.
3. Invite the children to smell each of the herbs.
4. Encourage them to taste the herbs.
5. After all of those in this first group have had an opportunity to smell and taste the herbs, invite other small groups of children to participate until all of the children have had an opportunity to do so.
6. At snack time, place the fresh vegetables and the variety of herbs on each of the snack tables. Encourage the children to make their own salads, seasoning them with the herbs to suit their own taste.

### NAME THAT SPICE (5 AND 6-YEAR-OLDS)

**Description of Activity**
　　The children make spice charts to use at home during Havdalah.

**Materials**
　　a variety of sweet-smelling spices (no pepper or paprika)
　　small paper cups (one for each of the spices chosen)
　　white typewriter or computer paper (at least one sheet per child)
　　white glue

# What's Missing

### Procedure
1. Gather a small group of children together around a table with all of the materials within easy reach.
2. Place each of the spices in a paper cup.
3. Discuss Havdalah, the importance of smelling pleasant spices at the ceremony, and ways that the group can prepare a spice chart for use at Havdalah.
4. Help the children to fold their papers carefully in half as many times as they wish. When they open their folded papers, they will have created as grid as shown below.

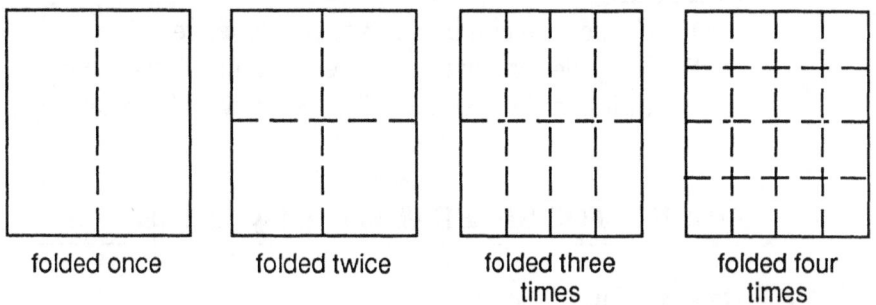

folded once    folded twice    folded three times    folded four times

5. Encourage the children to place a small drop of glue in each box.
6. They then select the spices to drop onto each of the drops of glue.
7. As the completed spice charts are set aside to dry (approximately 1/2 hours), gather together another small group of children and repeat the procedure.
8. After all of the children have had an opportunity to create a spice chart, gather the entire group together at circle time and encourage them to share their charts with the rest of the group. They can smell the others' charts and try to identify the spices.
9. The children may take their spice charts home for use there.

# Sing Along

### Goals
To help children become aware of each person's role in preparing for and celebrating Shabbat.

To help children understand that careful and caring preparation for Shabbat enhances its specialness.

## SINGING FOR SHABBAT (3 and 4-year-olds)

### Description of Activity
The children sit in a circle and sing a song. They take turns filling in words of their own choice at the end of the song.

### Materials
"Shabbat," on an audiotape entitled "I Live in the City" by Robyn Helzner (RAH Productions, POB 11398, Washington, DC 20008)

### Procedure
1. Gather the children together in a circle.
2. Sing the song over and over, encouraging each of the children to take turns filling in the last part of the song with their own choice of words.

## SINGING FOR SHABBAT (5 and 6-year-olds)

### Description of Activity
The children sit in a circle and, with the use of key words, create songs for Shabbat.

### Materials
"Shabbat," on an audiotape entitled "I Live in the City" by Robyn Helzner (RAH Productions, POB 11398, Washington, DC 20008)
two experience charts
felt markers

### Procedure
1. For several days during free play time, play the above-mentioned tape, making sure that the Shabbat song is heard many times.
2. Gather the children together in a circle and and tell them that they are going to create their own Shabbat song.
3. Ask the children to mention special words about Shabbat and write these words on one experience chart (e.g., Shabbat, *challah*, wine, *Kiddush*, candles, spices, Havdalah, *Z'mirot*, Cantor, Rabbi, praying, synagogue). Add words if desired.
4. Instruct each child to use one of the words on the experience chart to create a line for the song. The tune will be the Shabbat song on the tape.

5. As each child makes up a line to the song, that line is written on another experience chart.
6. After each child has a turn, the class can sing the class Shabbat song. This song can then be used at the class pre-Shabbat party, and copies may be sent home for use at the home Shabbat observance.

## TAKING THE STORY HOME

1. **Reading Stories**
   Suggest to parents that they read the following with their children:
   *Will I Have A Friend?* by Miriam Cohen
   *My Special Friend* by Floreva G. Cohen
   *Just Enough Room* by Miriam P. Feinberg
   During and after the reading, ask questions such as:
   What can you do to make a friend feel comfortable?
   Did you ever invite a friend to your house? What things did you do together?
   Did your friend have a good time?

2. **Shabbat Guests**
   a. During a weekday, the family can sit together while each member participates in telling a story (real or fictitious) about Shabbat guests. Each person contributes to the story while speaking into a tape recorder. It might be helpful for a parent to begin telling the story. After everyone has talked into the tape, listen to the story.
   b. Do this activity at the Shabbat dinner table without a tape recorder. Have each family member add to the story in turn.

3. **Shabbat Family Sing-along**
   Using the melody to *"Shabbat Shalom"* (also known as *"Bim Bam"*), each family member can make up her/his own words. Record the song on an audiotape. After all of the family members have sung onto the tape, it should be played back and listened to immediately and during future family times. Family members can make up chants to finish the sentence, I like Shabbat because . . . , and can add such things as the candles burn brightly, the *challah* tastes so good, the wine is sweet, etc.

CHAPTER 3
# The Stolen Donkey

## BEFORE TELLING THE STORY

People with pets often develop special relationships with them. Discuss the various pets children have and their feelings toward them. Then tell the story about a famous Rabbi and his pet — a donkey.

## TELLING THE STORY

Rabbi Hanina owned a donkey. He always took very good care of his pet. He gave the donkey oats to eat and water to drink.

One day, some thieves came into the Rabbi's garden and stole his donkey. They led him through the gate. They led him away, down the road, until they could no longer see Rabbi Hanina's house. They walked and walked, pulling the donkey behind them. At last, they came to their own house. They tied the donkey to a post so that he could not wander off.

"Let's feed the donkey," said one thief. They put a pile of oats in front of the donkey, but the donkey would not eat.

"That's strange," said another thief. "Let's give him water." But the donkey would not drink.

Day after day, the donkey would not eat and he would not drink. At last the thieves decided, "Let's get rid of this strange animal. He won't eat or drink. He could die. He's just not a good donkey." So they untied him, and chased him away.

The donkey had become weak from not eating or drinking. He was far from Rabbi Hanina's house. He wanted so much to get back home. He walked and he walked and he walked and he walked until at last he saw Rabbi Hanina's house. It was far, far off in the distance. As weak as he was, he managed to drag his tired legs and his weary body to the gate of Rabbi Hanina's house. There he stopped and lay on the ground. He was too tired to go any farther.

Rabbi Hanina was in his house with his family. Suddenly his daughter said, "Father, did you hear that? It sounds like our donkey braying." Everyone in the family listened for the sound.

"You're right!" shouted Rabbi Hanina. "Let's go outside and see where the braying is coming from." They ran outside as fast as they could.

Then they saw him. There lying on the ground was their donkey. He looked so weary!

Rabbi Hanina ran to get food for the donkey. His daughter scurried to find water. The donkey ate the oats. Then he drank the water.

Slowly, the donkey's strength returned. After a while, he was strong enough to walk to his home inside Rabbi Hanina's yard. It was good to be back home again with people who cared about him! He felt very happy!

*Questions on the Story*
1. Why wouldn't the donkey eat the food and drink the water that the thieves gave him?
2. How do you think Rabbi Hanina felt when he discovered that his donkey was gone?
3. What did Rabbi Hanina think had happened to the donkey?
4  Do you have a pet? How do you take care of your pet? What do you feed it?

## THEMES IN THE STORY

### The importance of caring for animals
Rabbi Hanina took good care of his donkey, and the donkey knew that his master cared about him.

*Bringing the Theme Closer*
- How do people care for their pets?
- How does your pet let you know when it needs something?
- How do you let your pet know that you care about it?

### Respecting the possessions of others
The thieves showed that they didn't respect Rabbi Hanina's possessions by stealing his donkey.

*Bringing the Theme Closer*
- How do you think Rabbi Hanina's donkey felt when strangers took him away from his home?
- Why was Rabbi Hanina worried about the donkey's safety?

## CREATIVE FOLLOW-UP

*Retelling the Story*

### Goal
To help the children sequence the events in the story.

### PICTURE-TELLING (3 AND 4-YEAR-OLDS)

**Description of Activity**
The children retell the story through the use of pictures.

**Materials**
pictures of donkeys laminated and mounted on construction paper
a bowl of oats, a bowl of water

**Procedure**
1. Gather 3 or 4 children together during free choice activity time.
2. Hold up one picture. Encourage a child to tell about the picture in relation to the story.
3. Then hold up another picture and ask another child to discuss it.
4. Continue this activity until all of the children have participated and all of the pictures have been discussed.
5. Place pictures in the order of the events as they occur in the story.
6. Repeat this activity with other small groups of children in the class.

### WALKIE-TALKIES (5 AND 6-YEAR-OLDS)

**Description of Activity**
The children retell the events of the story while using walkie-talkies.

**Materials**
string (one yard for each child)
paper cups (5 or 7 oz., two per child)
scissors (one per child)
transparent tape

**Procedure**
1. Gather a small group of children together during free choice activity time.
2. Give each child two cups and a piece of string.
3. After making a hole in the center of the bottom of the cup, each child places a piece of transparent tape on each end of the string and pushes one end through the bottoms of each cup.

Wrap end with scotch tape. Insert end through hole. Knot end inside cup.

4. Help the children remove the tape and make a knot at the ends of the string.
5. The walkie-talkie is now ready to use. One child holds one cup next to his/her ear while another walks with the cup as far as the string will go. The children can then take turns talking to each other through the cups. As one child talks into a cup, the other holds it up to his/her ear and listens.
7. Encourage the children to retell parts of the story by asking and answering questions about it. Examples of questions are:
   a. What kind of food does a donkey like to eat?
   b. Who came into Rabbi Hanina's yard?
   c. What did these people do?
   d. At the end of the story, what happened to the donkey?

## *Game Time*

**Goals**
To help the children understand how animals can communicate with each other.
To help the children understand that baby animals grow up to be adults, just as humans do.

## MATCHING BABIES AND GROWN-UPS (3 AND 4-YEAR-OLDS)

### Description of Activity
The children identify baby animals with full-grown animals through the use of pictures.

### Materials
pictures of:
a colt and a horse
a calf and a cow
a puppy and a dog
a kitten and a cat
a kid and a goat
a baby donkey and a full-grown donkey
a baby camel and a full-grown camel
construction paper (size and quantity to match that of the pictures of animals mentioned above)
white glue
scissors

### Procedure
1. Before meeting with the children, paste each picture onto a piece of construction paper which is slightly bigger than the picture.
2. Gather a small group of children together.
3. Show each picture to them and ask them to identify the animal and to state whether it is a baby or a grown-up.
4. Then place all of the pictures face up on the table.
5. Hold up one picture. Ask a child to identify the animal and to choose a picture of the same animal in its grown-up form.
6. Hold up another picture. Ask another child to identify the baby animal and to find a picture of the same animal as a grown-up.
7. Continue this activity until all of the children in the group have had a turn and all pictures have been identified.
8. This game can be repeated with several groups of children until all have had a chance to play.
9. When the children have become familiar with the pictures, place the pictures in a game box and encourage the children to play with them on their own.

## GUESS THE SOUND (5 AND 6-YEAR-OLDS)

**Description of Activity**
The children become aware of the different sounds that animals make.

**Procedure**
1. Gather a small group of children together. Make the sound of an animal and ask them to guess which animal you are imitating.
2. Then ask the children to take turns making sounds of animals they each choose to imitate. Give the child who guesses correctly an opportunity to make a sound for the others.
3. Continue playing this game with several groups of children until all of the children have had an opportunity to make and guess animal sounds.
4. As the game is being played, stop periodically and discuss why and how animals make certain noises (e.g., to communicate danger signals, to ask for food, etc.).

## *Food Experiences*

Goals
　To help the children prepare food in a careful and respectful manner.
　To provide interesting and inviting materials which will stimulate fine motor development.

## EDIBLE ANIMAL FACES (3 AND 4-YEAR-OLDS)

**Description of Activity**
The children create animal faces with food and then eat them for snack.

**Materials**
　at least one slice of bread per child
　softened margarine
　raisins
　celery sticks
　shredded cheese
　pitted cherries

**Procedure**
1. Gather a small group of children together and discuss ways in which food can be used to create edible pictures of animal faces.
2. Discuss the foods which you will make available and ways each can be used.
3. After encouraging the children to wash their hands, help them to make the following animal faces.

### A LION
a. Cut a large circle out of a slice of bread (use the rim of a glass like a cookie cutter).
b. Spread margarine on the circle.
c. Make a nose and eyes with raisins.
d. Create whiskers with celery sticks.
e. Create a mane with shredded cheese.

### A BEAR
a. Cut a large circle out of a slice of bread.
b. Spread margarine on the circle.
c. Make eyes with raisins.
d. Make a nose and mouth with pitted cherries.

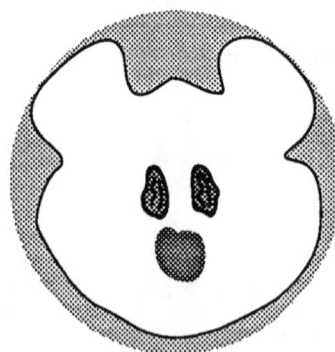

3. Recite the appropriate blessing before eating this snack:

*Baruch Atah Adonai Eloheynu Melech Ha-olam Hamotzi Lechem Min Ha'aretz.*

Blessed are You, Eternal our God, Ruler of the Universe, Who brings forth bread from the earth.

## EDIBLE ANIMALS (5 AND 6-YEAR-OLDS)

### Description of Activity
The children make animals from cookie dough and then eat them at snack time.

### Materials
ingredients for recipe below

### Procedure
1. Gather a small group of children together during free choice activity time. Encourage them to describe characteristics of animals (a tail, four legs, etc.).
2. Discuss ways in which the children can create animals from cookie dough.
3. Instruct them to wash their hands before beginning the activity.
4. Children make the dough according to the instructions below and shape it into animals.

*Gittel Schatzow's Sugar Cookies*
(An old family recipe contributed by her granddaughter, Rena Rotenberg)

### Ingredients
2 cups flour (minus 1 tablespoon per cup)
1/2 cup (or less) sugar
1 teaspoon baking powder
1 egg
1/2 cup oil
1 teaspoon honey
oil for greasing the cookie sheet

**Supplies**
- 2 large bowls
- 1 measuring cup
- measuring spoons
- large mixing spoon
- 1 small glass
- a cookie sheet
- a spatula
- a paper napkin for greasing the cookie sheet

**Method**
1. Mix the flour with the baking powder in a large bowl and set it aside.
2. Mix the oil with the sugar in a large bowl.
3. Add the egg. Observe the dietary laws here as follows:
   Break the egg into a glass cup. Then, with the participation of the children, examine the yolk. Discuss what constitutes an acceptable (kosher) egg, one without a blood spot.
4. Mix the egg with the oil and sugar.
5. Add honey and mix.
6. Add the flour mixture and mix well. When the dough comes away from the side of the bowl, it is ready.
7. Give each child a portion of dough and suggest that he/she create an animal shape. Discuss whether or not the animal has a tail, a large head, ears, etc.
8. Place the cookies on the greased cookie sheet.
9. Bake in 350 degree oven for 20 minutes or until golden brown.
10. Remove the cookies from the oven and let them cool. Eat them at snack time after reciting the appropriate blessing:

*Baruch Atah Adonai Eloheynu Melech Ha-olam Boray Minay M'zonot.*

Blessed are You, Eternal our God, Ruler of the universe, Who creates various kinds of food.

# TAKING THE STORY HOME

1. **Caring For Animals**
   If the family has a pet, encourage parents to discuss the concept of *tza'ar ba'alei chaim*, concern for living creatures. Pets must be fed before the family eats, since such animals cannot get food for themselves. Discuss ways in which pets communicate their needs to their owners and ways in which the donkey in the story above communicated his needs.

2. **Story Starters**
   Send home a list of story starters for the children to complete during carpool, at the dinner table, while taking a walk, etc.:
   Rabbi Hanina took good care of his donkey by . . .
   The thieves were not nice when they . . .
   The donkey wouldn't . . .
   The thieves were surprised that . . .
   Rabbi Hanina was in his house when . . .
   When the donkey came back home he . . .

3. **News Reports**

   **Materials**
   felt markers
   scissors
   a large gift box without a lid

   **Procedure**
   1. To make a "television screen," cut out the middle part of the bottom of the box so that a frame remains.
   2. Using a felt marker, draw control knobs on the box.

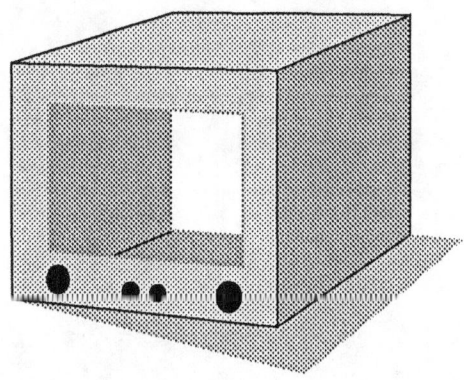

3. One family member pretends to be a reporter. The other family members take turns retelling the story to the reporter. The reporter and the interviewee place themselves behind the box so that it appears that they are on television. The other family members "watch television" until it is their turn to be interviewed. Interviewees assume the roles of Rabbi Hanina, his daughter, and anyone else who might have information which would be of interest to viewers on the theft of the donkey.
4. The interviewing can be resumed at later times with different family members and different story characters.

## CHAPTER 4
# *The Bell of Justice*

## BEFORE TELLING THE STORY

Discuss fairness. Consider why it is important and how it makes us feel when people act unfairly. Ask the children to suggest the best way to let others know when they feel they have not been treated fairly.

Display photographs of farm animals. Discuss the kinds of work that animals do. For example:
- dogs – provide friendship, guard, help the blind
- sheep – provide wool
- donkeys – pull carts and carry packages and people
- horses – pull carts and carry packages and people
- chickens – provide eggs
- cows – provide milk, pull wagons
- oxen – pull wagons and plows

## TELLING THE STORY

Once there was a king who lived in a little town. All of the people who lived in that town used to talk about how good and kind and honest their king was. The king especially wanted everyone to be treated well by others. To make sure that this would happen, he said to his people:

"Dear people, this is what I am going to do. I will build a tall tower in the middle of our city. It will have a large bell hanging in the belfry at the top. There will be a very, very long cord hanging from the bell to the ground. If anyone feels that he or she is not being treated fairly, that person should come to the tower and pull the cord. Then when the judges of the town hear the bell ring, they will come to the tower and decide what is right and how to make things more fair. I will call it the bell of justice."

The people were very happy with their king's decision. "We will try to be very fair with each other," they said. "But if we sometimes forget to be fair, the bell will be there for people to use. The bell will remind us."

And that was what happened. The bell and the town's judges worked very hard to help the people remember to be fair to each other.

But one day, the good king died. A new king ruled the city. He didn't care so much for justice. He didn't remind people about the bell. And soon, the people began to forget about their bell of justice. The long cord got thinner and shorter. After a while most people could not even reach it. And so the bell was no longer used at all.

It happened that a very rich and selfish and mean man lived in this town. This man owned a horse. Once this horse had been strong and fast. But when the horse grew older, he could no longer do hard work or run quickly. The rich man was disappointed in his old, slow horse.

"Go away, horse!" the mean man yelled. "I don't need you anymore. You can't work hard like you used to, so why should I waste any food on you?" And with that, the mean man opened the fence gate and chased the horse away.

The poor, sad horse wandered down the road. He looked here and there, there and here. He wished he could find something to eat. There was barely any grass on the ground. He wished there was some water somewhere to drink, but the river bed was completely dry. He wished he could find a new home, but no one seemed to want him. He wandered and stumbled, stumbled and wandered for many days.

One day the old horse came to the middle of an old city. Most of the buildings were all crumbled and broken. But there was a rather nice tower that was still standing. As the poor horse stood looking up at the tower, he noticed an old cord with ivy and green vines growing on it. He was so very, very hungry! He stretched his neck way, way up. He reached up as high as he could. Yes, he could reach the vine. Uhmmm, was it good. He nibbled on the vine, he chewed on the vine. Uhmmm, uhmmm, uhmmm. As he began to pull more of the vine off of the cord, he caught the cord between his teeth. He yanked on the cord. Suddenly, the old bell began to ring.

"What is that sound?" asked the younger people in the town. But the older ones remembered.

"Listen," said one. "I remember. That's the bell of justice?"

"Yes," said another. "We haven't heard it ringing for years."

And a third said, "Maybe someone needs justice. Let's call the old judges."

But the judges had already heard the ringing and were hurrying to the center of the town.

"Look!" called one judge, very disappointed. "It's only a horse trying to eat the vines. Let's go home." But as they started to leave, someone shouted, "This is the rich man's old horse. Remember how hard he used to work this horse? And now that the horse is old and weak, that mean man must have sent him away. Look how thin he is. The horse can't talk, but he can ring the bell to let us know he needs justice."

"Justice, justice," everyone shouted.

The judges went to find the horse's owner. "You have not treated your horse fairly," the judges told him. "Now you must pay a thousand gold coins. We will use this money to buy a stable and a pasture so that this horse will have a place to live for the rest of his life."

"And besides that," said another of the judges, "we are all very grateful to this animal for reminding us that we need to start using our bell again. This horse brought justice back to our town."

### Questions on the Story
1. What did the people of the town think about their first king?
2. How did the king feel about the people? How did he show his feelings?
3. How did the rich man treat his horse? What do you think about the way he acted toward the animal?
4. How did the horse remind the town people about their bell?
5. Have you ever heard bells ring? When and why do they ring?
6. Was the horse treated fairly in the end?

## THEMES IN THE STORY

***It is important to treat people and animals fairly.***

When the townspeople discovered that the horse was being treated poorly, they forced the rich man to pay gold coins to buy a stable and a pasture as a home for the horse.

*Bringing the Theme Closer*
- Have you ever felt unfairly treated? Did you let someone know about it? What did you do? Was there a change in the treatment because of what you did?
- Were you ever unfair to someone else? How did you feel then?
- Do you have a pet? How do you treat your pet? Does your pet have a way to let you know when something is wrong?

***It is important to find a way to express opposition to injustice.***
The townspeople remembered the purpose of the ringing bell and were happy to restore it to its original purpose when the horse caused it to ring.

*Bringing the Theme Closer*
- If you notice someone in school doing something that is not right, what should you do?
- If someone were to do something to you that wasn't right, what could you do? To whom could you go for help?

# CREATIVE FOLLOW-UP

## *Retelling the Story*

### Goal
To help the children understand the events of the story.

### BODY TALK (3 AND 4-YEAR-OLDS)

#### Description of Activity
Following the telling of the story, the children communicate ideas and events from the story without talking.

#### Materials
none

#### Procedure
1. Gather all of the children together in a circle.
2. Invite one child at a time to act out a part of the story without speaking.
3. The other children need to guess what that child is doing.
4. If the guess is correct, the actor nods his/her head. If not, he/she indicates a negative response.
5. Continue this activity until all the children have had a turn or until interest wanes.

## STORY IN A SACK (5 AND 6-YEAR-OLDS)

### Description of Activity
Following the telling of the story the children retell the story using props.

### Materials
a large paper grocery bag
various objects, such as a book, a *kipah*, pretend food, a picture of farm animals, a sun hat, and any other items which might relate to the story

### Procedure
1. Place all of the objects in the bag.
2. Choose one child to draw two things from the bag. These items will be used as props for acting.
3. The actor uses the items to act out a part of the story and the other children try to guess what is being told them through the actions.
4. When the others have correctly guessed the actor's message, another child is chosen to choose two items from the bag and to use them as props for acting out something about the story.
5. Continue this activity until all the children have had a turn or until interest wanes.

# *Art Activity*

## STORY CHARACTERS (3 AND 4-YEAR-OLDS)

### Description of Activity
The children make representations of the characters in the story.

### Materials
a roll of shelf paper or brown wrapping paper
felt markers
scissors
yarn
fabric pieces
pieces of gift wrapping paper
white glue

### Procedure
1. Gather together three or four children during free choice activity time.
2. Review the story with the children, with special emphasis on the characters, their clothing, occupations, and personalities.
3. One child at a time lies down on a large sheet of the paper.
4. Draw an outline of each child with a felt marker.
5. Each child creates a representation of a character from the story by cutting out their outline and decorating it with felt markers and other art materials. Characters include: good king, indifferent king, mean man, horse, judges, townspeople.
6. Suggest that each child talk about the character which he/she has chosen to represent. Ask: Why did you pick this character? What kind of a person/animal was the character? In what ways are you like or unlike the character you chose?
7. Upon completion of this activity, hang all of the representations on the classroom wall.

## CHARACTER REPRESENTATION (5 AND 6-YEAR-OLDS)

### Description of Activity
The children make representations of the characters in the story and dictate captions.

### Materials
pipe cleaners
toilet paper rolls
paper towel rolls
felt markers
yarn
white glue
masking tape
scissors

### Procedure
1. Gather together three or four children during free choice activity time.
2. Review the story with the children, with special emphasis on the characters, their clothing, occupations, and personalities.

3. Encourage the children to discuss the characters they have chosen to represent. Ask: Why did you pick this character? What kind of a person/animal was the character? In what ways are you like or unlike the character you chose?
4. As they describe the character, write captions on a piece of easel paper and place them near each representation.
5. Hang the representations on the classroom wall in the order in which they appear in the story.
6. Review the events of the story with the children, incorporating the caption at the bottom of each representation.

## *Listening Activity*

### Goals
To help the children to differentiate between different sounds.
To help the children to become aware of the various sounds in their world.

### CREATING SOUNDS (3 AND 4-YEAR-OLDS)

### Description of Activity
The children fill containers with different objects which create different sounds.

### Materials
many empty film canisters
4 bowls
Lego pieces
beans
rice
pebbles

### Procedure
1. Gather together 3 or 4 children.
2. Place all of the materials on the table. Place in each of the bowls one kind of material (i.e., Lego pieces in one, beans in another, rice in another, and pebbles in another).
3. Invite the children to fill a canister with a specific noisy item which they may select from the table. Then they place the tops on their canisters.

4. At circle time, all of the children who have made noisemakers can shake them in turn while the others describe the sound each makes and guess the contents.
5. Use the canisters to get the children's attention at transition time.

## WATER SOUNDS (5 AND 6-YEAR-OLDS)

### Description of Activity
The children fill bottles with differing amounts of water to make a variety of sounds when the bottles are struck.

### Materials
many small empty glass bottles of identical sizes
water
several funnels
a rhythm stick

### Procedure
1. Gather a small group of children together.
2. Show them the bottles and the water which have been set up for their use at a table.
3. Encourage them to pour water into the bottles, trying to fill them with different amounts so that no two bottles have the same amount.
4. After the bottles have been filled, invite children to take turns gently striking the side of each bottle with the rhythm stick. Help them to listen to the sounds and differentiate them.
5. Discuss the bottles and their sounds at circle time, giving each of the children a chance to create a melody for the others by gently striking the sides of the bottles with the rhythm stick.
6. Use the bottles to get the attention of the children at transition times.

# TAKING THE STORY HOME

### 1. Understanding Animals
Suggest to parents that when they take their children to the zoo, they can discuss the sounds made by the different animals. Also explore the role of the zookeeper — feeding the animals, caring for sick animals, and protecting them from harm. Relate this discussion to the story and the way in which the townspeople, in contrast to the mean man, cared for the horse.

2. **A Household Bell**
   Suggest that families buy a bell to use at home. Family members may wish to discuss appropriate times for using the bell (e.g., mealtime, bedtime, coming inside time, etc.).

3. **Story Starters**
   Send home a list of story starters for the children to complete during carpool, at the dinner table, while taking a walk, etc.:
   The good king of the town decided to . . .
   Every time someone in the town felt that he or she was not being treated fairly, he/she . . .
   A long time passed, and the bell . . .
   The rich man had a horse who . . .
   The rich man felt that the horse . . .
   When the people heard the sound of the bell, they . . .
   The judges looked at the horse and . . .

CHAPTER 5

# *Honi Ha-Meagel Sleeps for Seventy Years*

## BEFORE TELLING THE STORY

People feel very happy when they have done special things for friends or family members, or even for people they don't know. Ask the children to share experiences of ways in which they helped others or others helped them.

## TELLING THE STORY

A long time ago, there lived in Israel a man named Honi Ha-Meagel. He was a very wise man.

One spring day, Honi went for a walk. "What a lovely sunny day it is today," he thought to himself.

He noticed that there were people in the fields planting vegetables and fruit trees. As he passed by a pretty little house, he saw an old man planting a tree.

"Why would such an old man be planting a tree?" he wondered. "It takes a very long time for fruit trees to grow, and planting is hard work. He might not even be around when the tree is big enough to give fruit."

Then Honi said aloud, "Excuse me sir, but what kind of tree are you planting?"

"This sapling is a carob tree," said the man. "I love to eat carob on Tu B'Shevat. In about seventy years, this tree will produce carobs good enough for eating."

"Do you think that you will live seventy more years and be able to eat the carob fruit?" asked Honi.

The man looked surprised."Oh, no! But I remember seeing carob trees growing when I was a little boy. I ate some of those carobs on Tu B'Shevat. They were so delicious! Those carob trees were planted by those who wanted to leave a gift for younger people. I am planting this tree as a gift for the people who will be living seventy years from now. Then they can enjoy eating carob on Tu B'Shevat, too. Just as my parents and grandparents planted trees for me, so I plant trees for my children and grandchildren."

"That's a very smart thing to do," said Honi, and he continued his walk. After a short while, he began to feel very tired.

"I'll just rest for a few moments," he thought as he sat down on the ground. "Maybe I'll close my eyes for a while. I'll eat my lunch when I wake up."

Honi stretched out on the ground, closed his eyes and fell into a deep sleep. While he slept, a wonderful thing happened. A rock appeared nearby. It grew bigger and bigger. After a while, it began to surround Honi. Then it grew into the shape of a tent, with Honi inside. The tent protected him from the wind, from the rain, from the cold, and from the hot sun.

Honi slept very comfortably inside the tent. He slept on and on for a very long time. He slept during the winter. He slept during the summer. He slept when it was raining. He slept when the sun was shining. He slept and slept. He slept for seventy years!

One day, the tent that covered Honi began to shrink. It grew smaller and smaller until it did not cover him anymore.

Honi woke up. He looked around. He stretched and stretched.

"What a good nap I had!" said Honi, his arms out wide and his mouth yawning. "I must have slept for a long time."

Honi noticed a man picking carobs from a tree nearby. This man was not the one to whom Honi had spoken earlier.

Honi stood up and walked over to the man. "Did you plant this tree?" he asked.

"No," answered the man. "My grandfather planted it seventy years ago".

"I can't believe it," Honi said to himself. "I must have been sleeping for seventy years!"

"I'm going to plant a carob tree also," said the man. "See, I have a sapling all ready to plant. Someday my children and grandchildren will be able to enjoy carobs just as I do."

Honi remembered the words of the old man. "Just as my parents and grandparents planted trees for me, so do I plant trees for my children and grandchildren."

### Questions on the Story
1. What did Honi see as he went for a walk?
2. What do you think a carob tree looks like? (If possible, show a picture of a carob tree.)
3. Why was the old man planting a tree?
4. Why did this seem strange to Honi?
5. What happened when Honi lay down and closed his eyes?
6. How was Honi protected when he slept for seventy years?
7. What is the longest time you ever slept?
8. What did Honi see when he woke up?

## THEMES IN THE STORY

### *It is important to plant for the benefit of others.*
Honi observed an old man planting a tree knowing he would never be able to enjoy the fruit.

*Bringing the Theme Closer*
- Discuss the kinds of things which we enjoy doing for others. Why do we do them? How does it make us feel?
- What kinds of things do others do for us? Do we enjoy those things?

### *Some of the things we plant will benefit those who will live in the future.*
Honi spoke with a man who was enjoying the fruit of a tree planted by his grandfather.

*Bringing the Theme Closer*
- Discuss trees, their ages, who planted them, and the kinds of fruit that grow on them.
- What is your favorite fruit? Where did it come from? Who do you think picked it? Who do you think planted the tree from which it grew? How old do you think that tree was?
- Take a trip to the library with the children to look for other books about trees. Read stories to the children on the subject. Here are a few suggestions of appropriate stories:
  *Once There Was a Tree* by Phyllis A. Busch
  *Caring for Trees on City Streets* by Joan Edwards
  *Johnny Appleseed* by Steven Kellogg
  *Picture Guide to Tree Leaves* by Roy Wiggers

## CREATIVE FOLLOW-UP

### *Retelling the Story*

#### Goal
To help the children sequence the events in the story.

#### INTERVIEWS (3 and 4-year-olds)

#### Description of Activity
The children pretend to be Honi asleep. When they awaken, the teacher interviews them about what happened.

#### Materials
a rectangular block
experience chart
felt marker

#### Procedure
1. All of the children sit in a circle.
2. Gather three to six of them together in the center of the circle.
3. Suggest that each of those in the center of the circle pretend to be Honi sleeping for seventy years.
4. Wake them up one-by-one. The teacher interviews them, using the block as a pretend microphone. Ask such questions as: How old are you? How long do you think you slept? What did you dream about? Why do you think you slept for so long? etc.
5. Ask each interviewee to speak into the "microphone" as they answer questions about their lives and experiences as Honi.
6. Upon completion of this activity, those children should exchange places with the children sitting in the outer circle. The activity is then repeated as described in numbers 2-4 above.
7. Continue this activity until all of the children have had a turn to be Honi.

8. As the interviewees respond, record their responses on experience chart paper which is entitled "Our Class Newspaper."

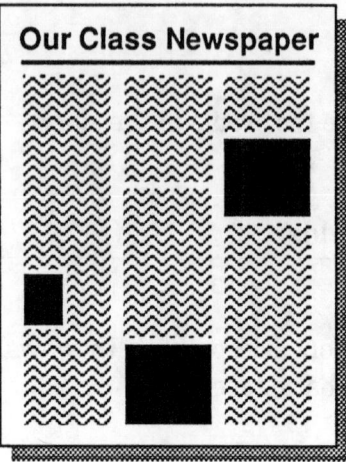

9. After the interviews have been completed and recorded on the experience chart, read the chart in its entirety with the children.
10. Display the class newspaper on a bulletin board so that the children may "read" it whenever they wish.

## INTERVIEWS (5 AND 6-YEAR-OLDS)

### Description of Activity
The children pretend to be Honi asleep. Upon waking, they interview each other about what happened.

### Materials
a rectangular block

### Procedure
1. All of the children sit in a circle.
2. Gather three to six of them together in the center of the circle.
3. Suggest that each of those in the center of the circle pretend to be Honi sleeping for seventy years.
4. Wake them up one-by-one. The teacher chooses a child to interview the sleepers about what happened as they slept. They use the block as a pretend microphone.

5. Ask each interviewee to speak into the "microphone" as they answer questions about their lives and experiences as Honi.
6. As the sleepers choose others to take the role of Honi, the interviewer chooses a new interviewee.
7. Continue this activity until all of the children have had a turn to be Honi.

## *Music and Dance*

### Goal
To reinforce the mental images associated with the characters in the story.

### SWING AND SWAY (3 AND 4-YEAR-OLDS)

**Description of Activity**
The children dress up as gardeners and move to the beat of the music.

**Materials**
scarves
sun hats
gardening tools
a song on a tape (suggestions: *"Hiney Mah Tov,"* "The Farmer in the Dell," "Here We Go 'Round the Mulberry Bush," or another song of your choice)

**Procedure**
1. Encourage the children to dress themselves in the scarves and sun hats and to use the gardening tools as they think the story characters might have used then.

### SWING AND SWAY (5 and 6-year-olds)

**Description of Activity**
The children act out parts of the story with background music as the teacher narrates.

**Materials**
a song on a tape (suggestions: *"Hava Nagila," "David Melech Yisrael,"* "Old MacDonald," or another song of your choice)

### Procedure
1. During circle time, discuss how the children can act out the story. Suggest that they volunteer for various parts; wind, sun, rain, the rock, the tent, carob trees, Honi, the old man, the young man.
2. The teacher begins to narrate the story with the background music playing softly. As the narration proceeds, the children act out their parts.
3. At a subsequent time, a child can be the narrator.

## *Food Experiences*

### Goal
To acquaint the children with the taste of carob, which is mentioned in this story, and which grows in abundance in Israel.

## SNACK TIME TREATS (3 AND 4-YEAR-OLDS)

### Description of Activity
The children make and drink a carob cocoa drink.

### Materials
Ingredients and supplies for the recipe below

### Procedure
1. The children help to make a carob cocoa drink according to the recipe below.

*Carob Cocoa*
(Reprinted with permission from *Recipes and Jewish Cooking Experiences For Pre-School Children* by Marsha R. Kargon, published by the Baltimore Board of Jewish Education, Baltimore, Maryland, 1983)

### Ingredients
1/3 cup carob powder
1/3 cup honey or sugar (or to suit taste)
1 cup water
2 tsp. vanilla
2 quarts milk
marshmallows or whipped cream (optional)

**Supplies**
1 large sauce pan
1 large bowl
1 wooden spoon
measuring cups
measuring spoons
cups

**Method**
1. Combine carob powder, honey, and water in a large sauce pan. Bring to a boil, stirring constantly.
2. Add vanilla and milk. Heat thoroughly, stirring constantly.
3. Serve hot with marshmallows or topped with whipped cream, or refrigerate and serve cold.

## MAKE CAROB TREATS (5 AND 6-YEAR-OLDS)

**Description of Activity**
The children make and eat a snack which combines healthful ingredients.

**Materials**
Ingredients and supplies for the recipe below
1 cup sunflower seeds
1 cup peanuts
several stalks of wheat (if possible)
several carob pods (if possible)

**Procedure**
1. Compare the ingredients in their ground and unground forms.
2. Encourage the children to taste each ingredient in ground and unground forms while comparing the taste. (Note that children below age five should not be given whole peanuts to eat.)
3. Children help to make Carob-Cocoa Fudge Balls according to the recipe below.

*Carob Cocoa Fudge*
(created by Rena Rotenberg)

**Ingredients**
1/2 cup peanut butter
1/2 cup honey
1/4 cup carob powder
1/2 cup wheat germ
1/4 cup chopped walnuts
1/2 tsp. vanilla
1/4 cup nonfat dry milk powder

**Supplies**
1 large bowl
1 wooden spoon
measuring cups
measuring spoons
1 square pan
1 sauce pan
a knife

**Method**
1. Heat peanut butter and honey in a sauce pan until mixture is thinned.
2. Remove from the heat. Add carob powder and stir with a wooden spoon until the mixture is smooth.
3. Add remaining ingredients. Stir or knead until the mixture is well blended. If it is too sticky, add more milk powder. If it is too dry, add some honey.
4. Spread fudge in a greased 8" square pan and chill in the refrigerator. Cut into small squares before serving. This fudge holds up well on picnics. Variation: Fudge may be shaped into small balls and rolled in ground nuts, dry milk powder, or sesame seeds. Chill thoroughly. Store in covered container in the refrigerator.

## TAKING THE STORY HOME

1. **Story Starters**
   Send home a list of story starters for the children to complete during carpool, at the dinner table, while taking a walk, etc.:
   When Honi went for a walk he noticed that...

He noticed an old man who was . . .
The old man loved carob because . . .
He was working hard planting so that . . .
When Honi fell asleep the strange thing that happened was . . .
Honi woke up after . . .
When he woke up he saw . . .
The young man told Honi that . . .

2. **Plant and Watch**
   Teach the children about how roots grow. Place an onion in a jar of water with the bottom half of the onion submerged. Draw a line on the jar with a red felt marker, indicating the location of the bottom of the root. Put the jar aside, and observe it on the next day to see if there is any growth. Again, draw a line on the jar with the felt marker, indicating the location of the bottom of the root. Continue this activity daily and observe the growth.

3. **Buy a Tree**
   Purchase a tree in Israel through the Jewish National Fund. Frame the tree certificate and place it in a prominent place.

CHAPTER 6

# *The Best Blessing*

## BEFORE TELLING THE STORY

Read *A Tree Is Nice* by Janice Udry. Lead a discussion with the children on why trees are nice.

Read *Trees Grow in Eretz Israel*, retold and translated by Ofra Reisman (World Zionist Organization, Department of Education and Culture in The Diaspora, Early Childhood Division, 1991). Discuss the foods that trees provide for us.

Ask the children to describe the ways we benefit from trees, and list their ideas on an experience chart as shown below.

> **Trees Help Us By...**
> 1. giving us fruit
> 2. giving us shade from the sun
> 3. giving us maple syrup

## TELLING THE STORY

There was once a traveler who was walking in the desert on his way to his home in Beersheva. He walked over many hills and through many of the valleys of Israel. He walked and walked all day long. He had nothing to drink or eat. He did not stop to rest. He had been traveling for quite a long time when he felt he could go on no longer.

He kept thinking to himself, "I hope I can find a place to rest. I wish I could find something to drink. I really need something to eat." But, where in the desert would he find such things?

Suddenly, as he got to the top of a small hill, he looked and saw a beautiful big tree very nearby. "What long, thick, green branches!" he thought, as he came closer to it. "And this is the most delicious looking fruit I've ever seen! And look at that brook with such clear, cool water running alongside the tree." He was just amazed. "This is perfect. Everything that I could ask for is here in one place!"

First he put his face into the brook and took a long drink. Then he washed his hands and face with the cool water. Then he ate some of the tree's delicious fruit. At last, he took off his sandals and lay down under the shady tree.

"This is wonderful," he said out loud. He began to smile and chuckle with delight. "The shade of the tree keeps me cool, the fruit from the tree is delicious, and the water that runs beside the tree is clean and refreshing." And, before he knew it, he was fast asleep. He slept for many hours.

When the traveler woke up, he felt very, very good. He stood up next to the tree that had given him shelter, shade, and food, and said out loud, "I must repay this wonderful tree. It helped me when I needed help. Now I will give the tree the best thing I can think of — a blessing."

But, what kind of blessing could he give to the tree? It wouldn't make sense to wish it long life. It was already a very old tree. It would be foolish to wish it delicious fruit. Its fruit was already very special. Would he wish it long branches with luscious green leaves? It already had those. Should he wish that its roots be bathed by a brook of fresh water? That, too, the tree already had.

Maybe the tree had everything. Maybe it didn't need a blessing.

Then he thought, "I have an idea. I wish ... that all trees planted from the seeds of this tree ... will be as beautiful and as blessed as this tree is."

And from then, on all the trees that grew from the seeds of that tree were as luscious and beautiful and special as the parent tree was.

### *Questions on the Story*
1. Why did the traveler walk home instead of getting there another way?
2. In what other way could he have gotten there?
3. Did you ever hear of the city of Beersheva? Do you know some names of other cities in Israel?
4. How did the tree help the traveler?
5. What gift did the traveler give to the tree?
6. Can you think of another gift to give to a tree?

## THEMES IN THE STORY

### *Trees are important for people*
When the hot, weary, and hungry traveler needed help, he turned to the tree which refreshed and fed him.

### *Bringing the Theme Closer*
- Have you ever been helped by a tree? How?
- Do you know of other ways in which we are helped by trees? What are they?

### *Blessings are prayers of thanksgiving*
The traveler's most appropriate gift to the tree was a blessing.

### *Bringing the Theme Closer*
- Do you know any blessings? Which ones?
- Can you say the blessing for bread? Can you say the blessing for fruit that grows on trees?
- What blessing would you give a tree?

## CREATIVE FOLLOW-UP

### Retelling the Story

#### Goals
To help the children sequence the events of the story.
To help the children understand the values shown in the story.

### SAY AND PLAY (3 AND 4-YEAR-OLDS)

#### Description of Activity
The children retell the story by acting it out with props.

#### Materials
a prop box (a small carton with a cover)
branches and leaves, real or made from paper and cardboard (for the children who pretend to be trees)
several blue scarves (for the children who pretend to be the brook)
a hat
a pair of sandals

# The Best Blessing

**Procedure**
1. Review the story with the children.
2. Show them the prop box and encourage them to take turns selecting something from it.
3. Each child selects an object, then uses it while pretending to be a character in the story. As many children may pretend to be trees as desired. Two children who pretend to be the brook can hold and wave the scarves.
4. Continue this activity until every child has had a turn.
5. After completion of this activity, place the box in the dramatic play area so that the children may continue using it during free choice activity time.

## TELL AND POINT (5 AND 6-YEAR-OLDS)

**Description of Activity**
The children take turns telling the story. At a signal from the teacher, the teller stops telling the story and then points to another child who will continue the story.

**Materials**
none

**Procedure**
1. Sit in a circle with the children and begin telling the story.
2. After a short time, stop and point to a child who will continue telling the story.
3. At a signal from you, that child will stop and point to another child who will then continue telling the story.
4. Continue this procedure until everyone has had a turn or until the story is finished.

## *Blessings for Fruits*

**Goals**
To introduce the blessings to recite 1) when eating fruits that grow on trees and 2) when drinking juice that comes from those fruits.
To help children learn the appropriate procedure for reciting the blessings.

### LET'S SAY THE BLESSING (3 AND 4-YEAR-OLDS)

**Description of Activity**
The children say the appropriate blessing for fruits.

**Materials**
a variety of fruits (apples, pears, peaches, oranges)
a paring knife
a bowl
a plate for each child
napkins

**Procedure**
1. Request that each child bring a fruit from home.
2. After collecting all of the fruits, instruct the children to wash their hands and come together to examine the fruits.
3. Examine the fruits with the children, noting differences and similarities (color, texture, size, the type of tree it grew on, etc.). Cut the fruit in half and discuss half and whole.
4. Tell the children about blessings. Explain that we say blessings to thank God for the sun and rain and soil so that the trees can grow and provide the good fruits that we like to eat.
5. Say the following blessing, encouraging the children's participation:

   *Baruch Atah Adonai Eloheynu Melech Ha-olam Boray P'ri Ha'eytz.*

   Blessed are You, Eternal our God, Ruler of the universe, Who creates the fruit of the tree.

6. Invite the children to eat the fruits.

### LET'S SAY THE BLESSING (5 AND 6-YEAR-OLDS)

**Description of Activity**
The children observe two different fruits, make juice from the fruits, recite the appropriate blessings, and drink the juice.

**Materials**
oranges
orange juice
apples

apple juice
juice squeezer
one cup for each child

**Procedure**
1. Gather a few children together at a table.
2. Show them the fruits and juices.
3. Discuss similarities and differences between the fruits and the juices which came from those fruits.
4. Cut the fruits in half and help the children to squeeze the juice from that fruit into a cup.
5. Before beginning to drink the juice, recite the blessing with the children, as follows:

    *Baruch Atah Adonai Eloheynu Melech Ha-olam Shehakol Neh'yeh Bidvaro.*

    Blessed are You, Eternal our God, Ruler of the universe, by Whose word all things come into being.

6. Help the children notice that the blessing for the juice is different from that for the fruit. Point out that the change in the blessings occurred when the fruit changed its form and became juice. Mention, too, that a different blessing is recited when drinking grape juice (...*Boray P'ri Hagafen*).

## *Watching Trees*

**Goals**
To help the children become aware of seasonal changes.
To note the changes in the trees during the school year.

### ADOPT A TREE (3 AND 4-YEAR-OLDS)

**Description of Activity**
The children observe the changes in a tree during the various seasons.

**Materials**
drawing paper
crayons
felt markers

### Procedure

1. Gather the children together and discuss the changes which could occur in trees over a period of several months (e.g., color and quantity of leaves, presence or absence of birds' nests, etc.). Ask them to select a tree which they can observe from the classroom window. If they cannot see one, go outside and select a tree close to the school building.
2. Indicate the day of the week on which the tree will be observed by marking the calendar with a sign of a tree on the same day each month
3. Make a point of observing the tree with the class each month on the chosen day.
4. Following the observation, encourage each child to draw a picture of his/her observation. Invite all to describe their pictures and to write down the description at the bottom of the page. Those children who can write should be encouraged to write their own descriptions.
5. Gather all of the pictures together to form a book to be taken home at the end of the school year.

## LEAF PRINTS (5 AND 6-YEAR-OLDS)

### Description of Activity

The children collect leaves and make leaf prints, then use the leaves for a variety of games that teach and reinforce matching skills.

### Materials

as many leaves as the children can gather on a walk in a wooded area
black tempera paint
several sponges
a large pack of 5" x 8" index cards
dark felt markers
a box (about the size of a shoe box)
clear Contact paper
a large spoon
a large paper bag for each child

### Procedure

1. Gather the children together. Provide each of them with a paper bag and go with them on a walk to collect leaves.
2. As the group walks in a wooded area, point out different trees and leaves with various shapes.

3. Encourage each child to look for several different kinds of leaves and to place them into the bag.
4. After the walk, gather together 3 or 4 children during free choice activity time. Help them to classify the leaves which they collected according to color, shape, and size.
5. Gather the children around a table on which all of the materials are placed.
6. Encourage the children to spread the paint on the back of each of their leaves with a sponge.
7. They then place the painted side of their leaves down onto a card, and press down on all parts of the leaves with a spoon.
8. Children remove the leaves from the cards, allowing the paint on the cards to dry.
9. Write the name of the leaf on the card which contains its print.
10. Carefully wash and dry the leaves.
11. When the leaves and the cards have completely dried, cover them with Contact paper.
12. Now the leaves and their corresponding prints can be used for a matching game or kept in a box until the children are ready to use them.
13. Continue doing this activity with other small groups of children until all of the children have had an opportunity to create leaf prints.

## TAKING THE STORY HOME

1. **Make a Popcorn Tree**
Suggest that family members make a popcorn tree using the following materials:
   newspaper
   colored construction paper
   food coloring (brown, green and other colors as desired)
   paper cups
   water
   plastic spoons
   glue
   pencils, crayons, or felt markers

   Everyone sits around the table and decides what kind of tree each person will make. Cover the table with newspaper. Using a writing implement, each person can draw a tree on a piece of construction paper. Combine water and food coloring of your choice in the paper cups. Drop popcorn pieces into the cups. Stir with the spoons, then remove the pieces from the cups. Allow them to dry on the newspaper. After the popcorn pieces have dried, glue them onto the construction paper, filling in the outlines of the trees. When all of the pictures are completed, display them as desired.

### 2. Visit a Garden

Visit an arboretum or a botanic garden. Notice the types of tree that are there and discuss their similarities and differences. Talk about the trees that are in your yard or neighborhood. If there are no trees there, perhaps it would be a good idea to plant one, care for it, and watch it grow.

### 3. Say Blessings

Family members can recite blessings for things that grow on trees. Send home a letter containing the blessing said before eating fruits that grow on trees (apples, oranges, grapefruit, etc.) and nuts (walnuts, cashews, etc.).

*Baruch Atah Adonai Eloheynu Melech Ha-olam Boray P'ri Ha'eytz.*

Blessed are You, Eternal our God, Ruler of the universe, Who creates the fruit of the tree.

Explain that bananas and pineapples are classified as "fruit of the ground," because the tree trunk or its branches wither or are cut off annually. If fresh seeds must be planted annually, the fruit of those plants are also classified as fruit of the ground. The blessing recited before eating those fruits is:

*Baruch Atah Adonai Eloheynu Melech Ha-olam Boray P'ri Ha'adamah.*

Blessed are You, Eternal our God, Ruler of the universe, Who creates the fruit of the earth.

CHAPTER 7
# King Solomon and the Bee

## BEFORE TELLING THE STORY

Discuss the importance of insects — what they do for us and their importance in nature. Emphasize the Jewish concept that all creatures in this world have importance.

Bring in books about insects. Read the books, show pictures of the insects, discuss them. Keep the books in the classroom library center.

## TELLING THE STORY

One very warm day, King Solomon sat in his garden in the shade of his fig tree. Being a very wise man, he spent a lot of time thinking.

He leaned his head back and thought, "It was a lot of work to build the Temple. But, I am proud that I have built the most beautiful building that anyone has ever seen. Now all Jews can come to Jerusalem to pray here. And now, I am so very, very tired. Maybe I'll just close my eyes for a moment and rest."

His eyes had barely closed when . . . Zzzzip! He felt a sharp pain on the tip of his nose. He was stung by an insect, and did it hurt!

He opened his eyes. He touched his nose. "It's getting bigger," he noticed. He touched his nose again. "Now it's getting hot!" he shouted.

He stood up quickly. "I want to find the insect that did this to me! Call all the bees and all the wasps and all the mosquitoes together," he commanded his helpers. "I want to find whichever one stung me, and right this minute!"

In just a few seconds, all the bees and all the wasps and all the mosquitoes were gathered in King Solomon's garden. Because he was so wise, he knew the languages of all the creatures on earth. There was nothing that the insects were saying that he didn't understand.

"Bzzz, bzzz, I wonder why we are here," said one bee. "Bzzz, bzzz, King Solomon looks very angry. I wonder what happened," said another.

"Quiet!" yelled King Solomon angrily. I want to know which insect dared to sting me." King Solomon pointed to his very red, his very hot, his very swollen nose.

It was very quiet. Not a bee, nor a wasp, nor a mosquito, nor even a person made a sound. Suddenly, a little bee stood in front of all the other creatures and said in a small, shy voice, "Bzzz, bzzz, I did it, your majesty. I'm the one."

"How dare you?" roared the king. "Are you not afraid of the king?"

"Oh, my goodness! I'm so sorry," apologized the bee in a meek manner. "I'm a very young bee. I don't have much experience yet. I sometimes cannot tell the difference between a nose and a flower. Your nose was so beautiful. I couldn't resist it."

When King Solomon heard this explanation, he was no longer angry.

Then the shy little bee said, "Who knows? Maybe one day I will be able to help you."

At that King Solomon laughed. "Ha, ha! So you think that the king will need your help? Fly away, little bee, now!"

The frightened little bee left as fast as it could. As she flapped her little wings, she could hear the loud voice of the king: "Ha, ha! Can you imagine a little bee helping a strong, powerful king?!" King Solomon made so much noise that all of the rest of the bees, and the wasps, and the mosquitoes flew away, too.

A few days later, the Queen of Sheba came to visit King Solomon. "I have heard that you are a very wise man," she said. "I want to find out just how wise you are. I will ask a very difficult question of you. If you can answer it, I will know that what people say about you is true. I will give a very beautiful gift to the Temple that you built for your people."

Then she called to her helpers, "Bring out seven bunches of flowers." At that, seven young women came forward, each carrying a bouquet of flowers. All of the bouquets had flowers of yellow and red and white. All of the bouquets looked exactly alike.

"King Solomon," said the Queen of Sheba. "Here are seven bouquets of flowers. Only one of them is real. Without touching or smelling them, tell me which one is real."

King Solomon looked, and he looked, and he looked some more. He looked still another time. Then he decided to look still once more! "It's very hard to tell which is real," he thought. Suddenly, he heard a very small sound. Bzz, bzz, bzz.

"Why, it's a bee," he thought. "That's the sound I heard a few days ago." Then he smiled, "Well, it's the same little bee that stung my nose."

The little bee buzzed around for a while. Then she stopped to rest on one of the flowers, and began to drink its nectar.

No one seemed to notice the little bee except King Solomon. "These are the real flowers, King Solomon," whispered the bee in a tiny voice.

"Ha, ha. This is the real bouquet!" shouted King Solomon.

"You are correct, King Solomon, and I shall give a very beautiful gift to your Temple as I promised," said the Queen of Sheba.

"Thank you, thank you, little bee," whispered the king to his new little friend. "You have helped me just as you promised you would. Now I know that even the smallest creature is as important as the biggest one."

As the little bee flew away, she sang a happy song to herself — "Bzzz, bzzz, bzzz." And she heard King Solomon laughing out loud — "Ha, ha, ha, ha."

*Questions on the Story*
1. What did King Solomon build in Jerusalem?
2. Where was King Solomon resting?
3. Why did he feel pain on the tip of his nose?
4. Why did King Solomon forgive the little bee that stung him on the nose?
5. Why did King Solomon laugh when the bee said that someday she might help him?
6. Was the bee able to help King Solomon? How?

## THEMES IN THE STORY

*All living creatures contribute to society*

King Solomon appreciated the contribution of the little bee that helped him determine which was the real bouquet of flowers.

*Bringing the Theme Closer*
- Can you think of animals which contribute to the well-being of society? Can you think of an insect which makes a contribution?
- What about ants? Do they contribute to our lives in some way? How? (Suggested answer: Ants model cooperative group living and the value of hard work.)

- Do you think size makes something or someone more or less important?
- Who do you think was more important, the little bee or King Solomon?

*Accept apologies and don't bear a grudge*

When the little bee realized that she had stung King Solomon's nose, she apologized. Then King Solomon was no longer angry. At a later time, that same bee came back to help King Solomon.

*Bringing the Theme Closer*
- Has anyone ever apologized to you for some wrong done to you? How did you feel? What did you say or do?
- Have you ever apologized to someone else? How did you feel when you did so?
- What does it mean to say, "I'm sorry"? Can you think of a special time of the year when we say "I'm sorry" for things we did to others throughout the year? (Suggested answer: Yom Kippur)

# CREATIVE FOLLOW-UP

## *Retelling the Story*

### Goals
To help the children sequence the events of the story.
To help the children understand the concepts in the story.

### ROLE PLAY (3 AND 4-YEAR-OLDS)

### Description of Activity
The children assume the roles of the story characters and enact the events of the story for each other.

### Materials
none

### Procedure
1. During circle time, encourage the children to act out the events of the story, giving each child an opportunity to portray a story character of his/her choice.

2. Begin to tell the story, and as a character is mentioned, the child who is representing that character assumes the role.
3. Repeat this activity any number of times, until each child is given an opportunity to role play all the characters.

### CHARADES (5 AND 6-YEAR-OLDS)

#### Description of Activity
The teacher demonstrates the procedure for playing charades by taking the first turn to act out a story character or event. He/she then encourages the children to take turns playing the game.

#### Materials
none

#### Procedure
1. During circle time, lead the children in a game of charades by silently acting out the role of a specific character or story event.
2. The first child to guess correctly the name of that character or to describe the event is chosen to act out the role of another character or story event.
3. The group then tries to guess what this child is acting out.
4. Repeat this activity until all of the children have had the opportunity to act out the role of a story character or event.

## *Sing and Swing*

### Goals
To help the children develop listening skills.
To encourage the children to react in a particular way to music.

### LISTEN TO THE BEAT (3 AND 4-YEAR-OLDS)

#### Description of Activity
The children recreate the story events through creative rhythmic activities.

#### Materials
assorted rhythm instruments (rhythm sticks, triangles, tambourines, drums, maracas, etc.)

## Procedure

1. Following the telling and retelling of the story, gather the children together in a circle and distribute a rhythm instrument to each.
2. Advise them to listen carefully to your voice and to respond with their instruments as you retell the story. For instance, when you speak slowly, they should provide slow background "music." When you speak quietly, they should provide quiet background "music," etc. Advise them that if they cannot hear you and you need to give them an instruction, they should watch to see if you signal them by raising your hand. When this happens, they need to place their instruments in their laps and wait for another instruction.

## LET'S BE BEES (5 AND 6-YEAR-OLDS)

### Description of Activity
The children listen to the music and pretend to be bees.

### Materials
a recording of *The Flight of the Bumblebee* by Tchaikovsky

### Procedure
1. After telling, retelling, and discussing the story, discuss with the children how bees fly, their destinations, etc.
2. Discuss *The Flight of the Bumblebee* and its composer.
3. Play the music and encourage the children to move as they wish as they pretend to be bees.

## *Exploring Nature*

### Goals
To help the children appreciate the importance of bees to the balance of nature.
To help the children understand that all creatures are important in some way.

## BEES AND BEEKEEPING (3 AND 4-YEAR-OLDS)

**Description of Activity**
The children learn about bees from a professional beekeeper. They relate what they know about bees to the story.

**Materials**
pictures of bees, flowers, and hives.
honey
a box of crackers
several bowls
plastic spoons

**Procedure**
1. Contact an apiary, zoo, nature center, or honey manufacturer to arrange for a demonstration of beekeeping. Be sure to advise the speaker of the age, knowledge level, and attention level of the children.
2. In advance, talk with the speaker about what will be discussed during the visit. Ask the speaker to bring honey for the children to taste.
3. Inform the children of the guest's upcoming visit. Provide some information on the work that he/she does with bees and ways that this relates to the story.
4. On the day of the visit, introduce the visitor who will describe his/her work and workplace, and talk about the ways people benefit from bees and honey.
5. Encourage the children to ask questions of the visitor.
6. After the guest leaves, review the discussion and relate it to the story.

## BEES AND BEEKEEPING (5 AND 6-YEAR-OLDS)

**Description of Activity**
The children learn about bees from a professional beekeeper. They relate what they know to the story, writing their comments on experience chart paper. Invite the children to draw pictures that correspond to the comments recorded.

**Materials**
experience chart paper
felt markers

### Procedure

1. Contact an apiary, zoo, nature center, or honey manufacturer to arrange for a demonstration of beekeeping. Be sure to advise the speaker of the age, knowledge level, and attention level of the children.
2. In advance, talk with the speaker about what will be discussed during the visit. Ask the speaker to bring honey for the children to taste.
3. Inform the children of the guest's upcoming visit. Provide some information on the work that he/she does with bees and ways that this relates to the story.
4. On the day of the visit, introduce the visitor who will describe his/her work and workplace, and talk about the ways people benefit from bees and honey.
5. Encourage the children to ask questions of the visitor.
6. After the guest leaves, review the discussion and relate it to the story.
7. Write the children's comments on the experience chart.
8. Invite the children to take turns drawing pictures on the experience chart to correspond to the comments recorded.
9. Display the chart(s) and invite the children to add to it (them) as they wish following the completion of this activity.
10. If desired, bake a honey cake or prepare other dishes that make use of honey.

## TAKING THE STORY HOME

1. **Taste Honey**
   Buy a variety of kinds of honey. The family can spread each on a cracker and have a "honey tasting." Compare taste, color, and texture of each sample.

2. **Make a Honey Treat**
   Peel and cut up 4 oranges and 6 figs. Place the pieces in a bowl. Drizzle honey on the fruit and mix it all together. Let it stand for a few moments. Taste it. If desired, add other kinds of fruit.

3. **Watch Bees**
   Visit an apiary to observe bees in a natural habitat. Visit beekeepers who display beehives and sell honey.

# CHAPTER 8
# *Nicanor's Door*

## BEFORE TELLING THE STORY

Take the children on a visit to a synagogue sanctuary. Notice its special decorations: stained glass windows, doors, curtain/door in front of the Ark, etc. Discuss each of the decorations with the children.

If your school is housed in a synagogue, get permission to decorate the chapel or the sanctuary. Children can make decorations for their Friday morning service. Afterward, they can take the decorations home.

## TELLING THE STORY

Jewish people in Israel and all over the world were very excited. They had begun to build their Temple in Jerusalem, and it was going to be very beautiful.

The Temple was going to need many things, and everyone was eager to help in any way that they could with the building. Some people were at work building the walls. Some were busy carving columns. Some were at work on the ceiling and the roof.

When Nicanor of Alexandria heard the exciting news, he wondered, "What can I do to make the Temple even more beautiful? Such an important place for the Jewish people needs to be really, really special."

He thought for a very long time until he came up with an idea. "I know. I'll have two fantastically beautiful doors built here in Alexandria, and I'll send them to the Temple in Jerusalem." So Nicanor searched throughout Alexandria. He searched throughout Egypt. He searched everywhere. At last, he found craftspeople who knew how to make things out of wood and copper, objects that were more beautiful than anyone could imagine.

The craftspeople agreed to make two doors for the Temple. They promised that these doors would be more beautiful than anything anyone had ever seen.

Nicanor visited the people in their shop everyday and watched them as they worked. He didn't want to miss watching them for a single day.

The men and women worked on the doors for a very long time. They worked slowly and patiently. They didn't want to make a mistake.

# Nicanor's Door

At last, the doors were finished. Nicanor was amazed. He was very excited to see the beautiful wood and cooper doors.

"These doors are perfect for the new Temple," he exclaimed. "They have gorgeous designs in them! They are perfect in every way. Now, I need to make sure that nothing happens to them."

Carefully, Nicanor wrapped each of the doors separately in cloth. The doors were now ready for the long trip to Jerusalem. Nicanor took them down to a ship which would carry the doors to Israel. He watched as the doors were lifted onto the ship. Then Nicanor also got on the ship.

When all was ready, the ship left on its journey. The ship moved very, very slowly as it carried the heavy doors to their destination.

"This will be a long trip," Nicanor thought, "because the heavy doors are making the ship move more slowly than usual."

Several days after the ship had left the port, the sky suddenly grew dark. A wind began to blow. It blew harder and harder.

As the wind became very strong, the waves rose higher and higher. The large waves began to toss the ship around in the sea. The sailors were afraid.

"What should we do?" shouted one worried sailor.

"Those heavy doors are weighing us down," called another as the waves crashed over the deck of the ship. "Let's throw them overboard and save our lives." And with that, a group of sailors grabbed one of the doors.

"No, no!" shouted Nicanor. "You mustn't throw my beautiful door overboard." He tried to grab the door, but he was too late.

"You won't get my other door," cried Nicanor, as he ran to protect it. "If you throw this door over, you'll have to throw me, too." The sailors stopped, looked at each other, and shrugged their shoulders. Suddenly, an unusual thing happened. The storm stopped. The sea became calm. The sun came out and the sky turned light blue.

"At least I saved one of my doors," sighed Nicanor, as he wondered what might have happened to the other one.

The ship continued calmly on its trip. When it reached Israel, it docked at Acco. Nicanor watched as his beautiful door was carefully carried off the ship.

"Where is my other beautiful door?" he wondered. "The doors are a pair that need to be together."

As he thought, Nicanor heard a sound. "Whoosh, Whoosh", it went. Then it sounded even louder, "WHOOsh, WHOOsh." And then it grew even louder, "WHOOSH! WHOOSH!"

Nicanor ran to the place from which the whooshing sound was coming. The sailors ran after him. They all looked.

Beside the boat, floating on the gentle waves, was the missing door. It was still in the cloth that Nicanor had wrapped around it. "My door, my door!" shouted Nicanor, and he jumped and danced and sang. Even the sailors were happy. They jumped and danced and sang with him.

No one ever knew how the door found its way to Israel, but it didn't matter. Nicanor followed his doors as they were carried on wagons to Jerusalem. He stood nearby and watched as they were placed in the Temple.

Many people came to look at the beautiful new Temple. Nicanor listened as one person said, "Look at those beautiful doors. They are really special." And another said, "What a wonderful gift Nicanor gave to the Temple."

Nicanor was proud and happy.

Many years later, all the Temple doors were replaced with golden doors, except for Nicanor's doors. Nicanor's doors stayed in their place as a reminder of the miracle that happened on their trip from Alexandria to the Temple in Jerusalem.

### *Questions on the Story*
1. Why were Jews all over the world happy?
2. What were some of the things the Temple needed?
3. Of what were Nicanor's doors made?
4. How did Nicanor get his doors to Jerusalem?
5. Why did the sailors want to throw Nicanor's doors into the sea?
6. Where did Nicanor find the door that was lost?

## THEMES IN THE STORY

### *The importance of the Temple to the Jewish people*
Both the First and the Second Temple were of vital importance to Jews in Israel and throughout the world.

*Bringing the Theme Closer*
- Have you ever heard people talk about the Temple in Jerusalem? (Explain to the children that that Temple no longer exists today. When we go to Jerusalem, we can pray at the Western Wall, which is adjacent to where the Temple once stood).
- Have you ever heard people talk about the *Kotel*? (Explain that this is the Hebrew term for the Western Wall.)
- Do you know anyone who has visited Jerusalem and the *Kotel*?

### *Making a good deed even better*
Nicanor was a good man who wanted to contribute to the beauty of the Temple by providing it with the most beautiful doors possible. He therefore called together the best craftspeople he could find to enhance the holiest place on earth for Jews.

*Bringing the Theme Closer*
- What other things do you think people might have done to make the Temple more beautiful?
- What do people do today to make synagogues more beautiful?

### *The completion of tasks has rewards*
Nicanor saw his project through from beginning to end: he chose the best craftspeople to make the doors, he accompanied the doors on their journey across the sea, and he saw them to their final destination in Jerusalem.

*Bringing the Theme Closer*
- Have you ever made something that took a lot of work to finish?
- How did you feel when it was finished?
- How did you feel when you didn't finish something?

# CREATIVE FOLLOW-UP

## *Retelling The Story*

### Goals
To help the children sequence the events of the story.
To help them understand the story events.

### SHOW AND TELL (3 AND 4-YEAR-OLDS)

#### Description of Activity
As you retell the story, the children are encouraged to act out the events with the use of blocks, pieces of wood, a boat, and a water table.

#### Materials
a table
a water table
enough water to fill the water table halfway
a piece of wood that will float
a toy boat that will float
blocks (at least 20)
small wooden or plastic people (Fisher-Price or any other brand)

#### Procedure
1. Set up the wood, the boat, and the toy people on a table. Place the blocks at the other end of the table.
2. After the water has been placed in the water table, gather the children together in a circle and begin to retell the story.
3. As you start telling of the rebuilding of the Temple, designate a few children to pretend to rebuild the Temple with the blocks on the table.
4. As the story is being told, children who have been selected to do so act out that part of the story with the use of appropriate props.
5. After the story has been told in this manner, retell it with a child assuming the responsibility of the narrator and different children participating in demonstrating various parts of the story.

## LET'S ASK NICANOR (5 AND 6-YEAR-OLDS)

### Description of Activity
The children take turns conducting an interview with a child who assumes the role of Nicanor.

### Materials
a bathrobe
a chair

### Procedure
1. Gather the children together in a semi-circle. Tell them that Nicanor will come to visit them and that he will be happy to be interviewed and respond to their questions.
2. Then discuss several possible questions to ask, as well as the information which they would like to have on Nicanor (e.g., where he lived, what his life was like, why he decided to have the doors made, how he felt about the rebuilding of the Temple, etc.).
3. Choose a child to be Nicanor. This child wears the robe and sits on the chair on the center of the semi-circle.
4. Invite the children to ask questions of "Nicanor" and "Nicanor" to answer them.
5. Continue this activity until there are no more questions or until the children lose interest.
6. Repeat this activity at a later time, giving other children an opportunity to assume the role of Nicanor and to act as interviewer.

## *Obstacle Course*

### Goals
To help the children understand the specialness and centrality of Jerusalem to the Jewish people.

To give the children an understanding of the many obstacles that people overcame in their desire to reach Jerusalem.

## GOING TO JERUSALEM (3 AND 4-YEAR-OLDS)

### Description of Activity
The children pretend to go to Jerusalem by using an obstacle course in the classroom

### Materials
a large representation of two doors
chairs
blocks
tables
ropes
any other materials which seem appropriate
construction paper
felt marker
masking tape
stickers or mailing labels on which can be written "You're a winner" (at least one per child)

### Procedure
1. Create and display two large decorated doors on a bulletin board.
2. Using the materials mentioned above, set up an obstacle course that ends at the bulletin board.
3. During circle time, explain ways to use the obstacle course. Make signs with arrows pointing in the directions you wish the child to go. Place the signs at appropriate places along the obstacle course.
4. Have the children take turns going through the obstacle course.
5. Discuss the obstacle course as a representation of the road to Jerusalem and to the Temple, with the doors which are displayed on the bulletin board representing Nicanor's doors in the Temple.
6. During free choice activity time, encourage the children to pretend once again to "go to Jerusalem" by traversing the obstacle course. They can do this at their own pace and whenever they wish during this time.
7. The obstacle course can remain standing until all of the children who wish to use it have done so.
8. When each child completes the course, place a sticker on his/her shirt.

## JUMP-THROW GAME (5 AND 6-YEAR-OLDS)

### Description of Activity
The children pretend to travel down the road to the Temple in Jerusalem by completing certain physical activities which are shown to them through pictures.

### Materials
shelf paper
poster board
scissors
white glue
pictures showing activities (see below)

### Procedure
1. In one area of the classroom or in a large room reserved for gross motor activities, draw the lines for a jump-throw game on the shelf paper.
2. Draw the picture of the two doors adjacent to the square containing the number 7, as shown in the illustration below.

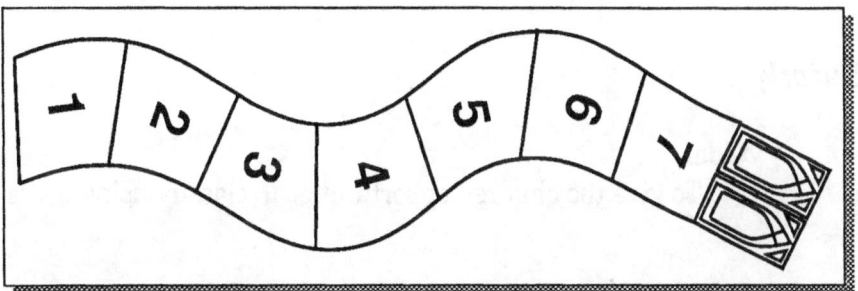

3. Photocopy and cut out the pictures below (showing activities such as sitting, jumping, hopping on one foot, tapping one's head with both hands, standing with hands on hips, placing hands on head while standing on one foot, etc.)

4. Glue the photocopied pictures onto poster board which has been cut to the size of the pictures. Place some of the cards into each of the boxes drawn on the shelf paper.
5. Explain to the children that you want them to help you pretend that the game board is the road to the Temple in Jerusalem. The box containing the number 7 is the Temple, and the picture of the doors represent Nicanor's doors.
6. Each child takes a turn as follows:
   a. When it is a particular child's turn, he/she stands facing the box containing number 1 and jumps into that box. The child picks up a card in that box and performs the activity shown on the picture. He/she then places the card back where it was found.
   b. The child then jumps into the next box, picks up a card, performs the activity indicated on the card, and places the card back in its place. He/she continues in this manner, going through all of the numbers.
   c. When number 7 has been reached, the child pretends to have reached the Temple and can touch the door.
   d. Now it is someone else's turn to pretend to reach the Temple and touch the door.

## Art Activity

### Goal
To give the children opportunities to classify using doors as the focus.

### DETAILS ON DOORS (3 AND 4-YEAR-OLDS)

**Description of Activity**
The children study doors and note similarities and differences (types, decorations, colors).

**Materials**
experience chart
felt marker

**Procedure**
1. After telling the story, inform the children that they will be going on a walk through the school to examine the doors in the building. They should

take particular note of the following:
How many doors are there in the school building?
What colors are they?
In what ways are they similar or different (with fancy decorations or not, with windows or not, with locks or not, etc.)?
2. During the walk, note the children's observations on a piece of paper.
3. Upon returning to the classroom, help the children to reconstruct the information that they acquired on their walk by creating an experience chart, such as the following:

> **Doors in Our School**
> We went for a walk in our school.
> We looked at all the doors in our school.
> We came into our school through a very big door.
> The door has a big lock.
> The door is brown.
> The door to our classroom has a window in it.
> The door is gray.

## DETAILS ON DOORS (5 AND 6-YEAR-OLDS)

### Description of Activity
After careful observation, the children describe doors.

### Materials
experience chart
felt markers

### Procedure
1. Follow instructions outlined in 1 and 2 above.
2. Upon returning to the classroom reconstruct the information acquired on the walk by creating a chart, such as the one found on the following page.

| Doors | | | | | |
|---|---|---|---|---|---|
| How many? | Colors | Windows | Locks | Location | With Mezuzah |
| | | | | | |

## *Creating*

### Goals
To encourage the children to think and use a variety of materials in creative ways.

To encourage the children to appreciate variety in techniques and products.

### MAKE NICANOR'S DOORS (3 AND 4-YEAR-OLDS)

**Description of Activity**
The children decorate a door as they wish.

**Materials**
a piece of shelf paper as long as desired
felt markers

**Procedure**
1. Roll the paper out on the floor and on it draw rectangular shapes of different sizes.
2. Invite each of the children to draw in each rectangular shape (or more than one if they wish to do so) to create a door that looks like Nicanor's door might have looked.
3. When everyone has had an opportunity to participate in this project, display it at the children's eye level.
4. Discuss similarities and differences in the various representations.

## MAKE NICANOR'S DOORS (5 AND 6-YEAR-OLDS)

### Description of Activity
The children use shoe box tops to recreate Nicanor's doors as they imagine them to have looked.

### Materials
shoe box with a lid (one for each child)
wire
pipe cleaners
beads
buttons
yarn
pieces of ribbon of various colors
white glue
scissors

### Procedure
1. During free choice activity time, invite a group of 3 or 4 children to work together at a table.
2. Provide the materials and explain that the lids of the shoe boxes will represent doors.
3. Encourage the children to decorate the lids in any way desired.
4. Make two holes along one of the long sides of each shoe box lid, and along the corresponding side of the shoe box.
5. Attach the lid to the shoe box with wire which is wound through the holes.
6. Stand the shoe box up on one of the shorter sides. Open and close the newly created "door."

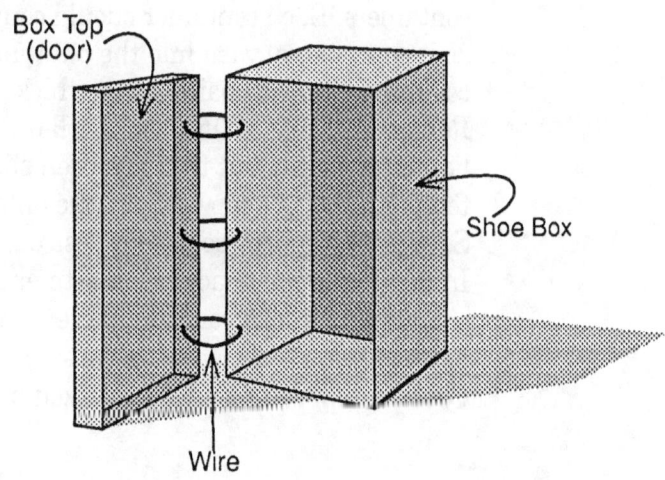

## TAKING THE STORY HOME

1. **Story Starters**
   Send home a list of story starters for the children to complete during carpool, at the dinner table, while taking a walk, etc.:
   Nicanor was excited because . . .
   He decided to help with the building of the Temple by . . .
   He hired some people to . . .
   Nicanor was worried about his doors when . . .
   His doors were so beautiful that . . .
   The Temple looked very . . .

2. **Decorating Doors**
   Suggest to parents that they and their children retell the story of Nicanor's door to each other. Following the retelling of the story, make a hanging to decorate a door in the house for each holiday of the Jewish year. Proceed as follows: Family members meet to decide upon the design for a particular holiday and to assign tasks to specific people. For example, very young children can make a collage, while older ones can do more intricate cutting, drawing, and decorating. When a plan has been made and tasks have been assigned, it is time to begin the project. Use a variety of craft ideas. (It might be helpful to visit a synagogue or school library or a Hebrew bookstore to find a book with craft suggestions.)
   - Blow-Out Pictures – Pour liquid tempera paint into a small shallow container. Dip the end of a plastic straw into the paint. Quickly transfer the straw to a sheet of paper and blow out to create interesting designs. If desired, fold the paper in half while the paint is still wet. When it is opened again, it will look different.
   - String Pictures – Pour liquid tempera paint into small shallow containers. Each container should contain a different color. Dip a string or piece of yarn into the paint and use it to draw designs on colored paper. The paint can be thickened with white glue if desired.
   - Roll-on Painting – Rinse out a roll-on deodorant bottle and fill it with liquid tempera paint that has been slightly thickened with powdered tempera. Roll the top of the bottle onto construction or drawing paper. Several bottles can be used if desired, each containing a different color.
   - Ironed Pictures – Place an assortment of items such as crayon shavings, pieces of yarn and pieces of ribbon on a large sheet of waxed paper. Create a design with the small loose items on the waxed paper. Cover with a second sheet of waxed paper of the same size. Place a

cloth over the materials and apply a warm iron to it. After the iron has been applied for some time, remove it and the cloth. Hold the waxed paper project up to the light to observe the colors and designs.
- Liquid Starch Painting – Apply liquid starch onto construction paper with a paint brush. Then apply layers of colored tissue paper to the sticky surface. Allow it to dry.

3. **Sailboats**

Each family member can make a sailboat as follows:

**Materials**
toothpicks
writing paper
walnut half shells
bottle caps
small jar lids or bottoms of small paper cups
modeling clay or play dough
scissors

**Procedure**
1. Each participant can decide whether to use a walnut half shell or paper cup for the boat.
2. Place a small mound of clay in the bottom of the boat.
3. Cut a triangle out of the paper to use as a sail.
4. Stick the toothpick into the sail at points noted in the diagram below.
5. Stick the sail into the clay.

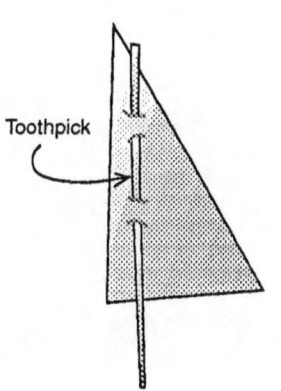
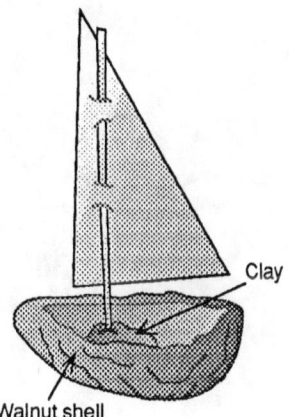

6. Place the boat into a pan of water and blow it across the water.

4. **Keeping the Synagogue Beautiful**
Suggest that family members discuss ways to help keep their synagogue beautiful. Make a list and display it on the refrigerator. Some ideas are as follows:
- Pick up papers that are lying on the floor or outside of the building.
- Put *kipot* that are on the floor or out of place back where they belong.
- Make sure that the prayer books are put away carefully and neatly.

**CHAPTER 9**

# Three Loaves

## BEFORE TELLING THE STORY

Discuss with the children the importance of being prepared to help others when they are in need. Solicit information from them on ways that others might need help and what we can do to help them. Write this information on an experience chart as shown below:

**Things we can do to help others:**
1.
2.
3.
4.
5.
6.

## TELLING THE STORY

A long, long time ago, during the days of King Solomon, there lived a woman named Judith. Even though Judith had very little money, she was always ready to help the poor people of Jerusalem. She worried about them. She wondered if they had enough to eat and a place to live. Each day Judith baked bread. She gave two loaves to the poor and kept one for herself to eat.

It happened one day that just as Judith had taken the loaves out of the oven and was placing them on the table to cool off, she heard a knock at the door.

"Rap, rap, rap," it went. With a loaf of bread still in her hand, Judith ran to the door and opened it. A very sad looking man stood there.

"Would you please be kind enough to give me something to eat?" he cried. "I am very hungry. I haven't eaten for three days. I was on a sailing ship. Suddenly a storm came up and all of the passengers were tossed here and there, up and down and all around. I fell overboard. Lucky for me, I was washed ashore."

"Here, take this loaf of bread," offered Judith, placing the bread in the poor man's hand. "It just came out of the oven."

"Oh thank you, thank you," smiled the man. "You are such a good person." And he waked away eating the bread.

"My goodness!" Judith thought. "I haven't even had breakfast yet." So she sat down in her kitchen and was preparing to eat one of her loaves when she heard, "Rap, rap, rap."

With the bread still in her hand, she walked quickly to the door and opened it. A young man was standing there. He looked thin and pale, very tired and hungry.

"Please, Ma'am, can you spare something for me to eat? I am so hungry. Some bandits overtook me on my way to Jerusalem. They took all of my money and all of my food. They even took my donkey. I have been walking for two days and I haven't eaten in a long time. I must have just a little something to eat," he explained.

Upon hearing this, Judith handed him the loaf of bread which she was holding. "Take this. I just finished baking it. I think you'll like it."

"You are so kind," smiled the young man, nodding his head while chewing big bites of bread. "I will never forget your kindness."

"Now, at last, I can eat my breakfast," Judith said out loud. She had barely sat down to her table when once she again heard, "Rap, rap, rap," at her door. Again she opened it and saw a woman and a child standing there. They did not look happy.

"Can you please give us something to eat?" asked the woman. "We were in the forest gathering berries when we lost our way. We wandered for a few days until we found our way here. We don't need very much, just a little food."

"Well, I just happened to be holding this loaf of bread when you knocked on the door," explained Judith. "So why don't you take it? I'm sure you'll enjoy it. It's freshly baked."

"Oh, thank you for being so kind. I hope we will be able to repay you some day," smiled the woman. And she hugged her child as they walked away eating the bread.

"Well, well. What will I have for breakfast now?" Judith wondered. "All of my loaves are gone, so I'll have to bake some more."

But when Judith looked in her flour sack it was empty. "Oh, well," she thought. "I have a little grain left and just enough money to pay the miller to grind it into flour."

"Please grind this wheat into flour for me," she said to the miller. "I need to make bread for my breakfast." So the miller ground all of her wheat, and put the flour into her flour sack. Soon Judith was on her way home to bake some more loaves.

As she walked along carrying her sack, a sudden gust of wind came up and blew the sack out of her hand. She tried to catch it, but she couldn't. "Oh, no," she started to cry. "What will I do now? I don't have any more grain. I don't have any more flour."

And then she got an idea. "I'll go to see King Solomon. He is very wise. Maybe he can help me."

So she walked to King Solomon's beautiful palace in Jerusalem. Soon she stood before him.

"King Solomon, I have a problem and I have come to ask for your help," she said. "I am really angry at the wind. It blew my sack away, and now I have no flour left."

As she was explaining what had happened to her, three sailors came bursting into the room. "King Solomon, a most wonderful thing has happened. We were at sea when our ship started to leak. It had a hole in its side that we could not close up. We tried everything we could think of, but nothing helped. The water kept coming in and the ship started to sink. We could only hope for a miracle. Then, all of a sudden the hole in the ship closed up. Water stopped coming in and we made it to port. When we checked the hole, we found that it had been closed by a sack. This sack saved us!"

The sailors held up the sack. They waved it around for all to see. "This sack saved our lives!" they shouted, with happy grins on their faces.

"Now we want to help others," explained another of the sailors. "We are so grateful for being saved that we want to give these coins as *tzedakah* to help someone else."

"That's my sack!" whispered Judith. "That's my flour sack that the wind carried away," she shouted, as she took it out of the sailor's hands.

"Here, then, take these coins, dear lady," offered the three happy men. "The coins are yours. Your sack saved us and everyone else on our ship."

"Yes," agreed King Solomon, "you should take the coins, Judith."

So, Judith did. On her way home, she bought flour with the coins. When she got home, she baked bread — three loaves. One she ate immediately, but the other two she gave away to those who were in need.

**Questions on the Story**
1. What did Judith do each day?
2. Why did she bake three loaves of bread?
3. Why was she so concerned about the poor?
4. What did Judith do when she ran out of flour?
5. What saved the sailor's ship?

## THEMES IN THE STORY

### *Hospitality*

Judith was hospitable to all of the people who came to her door asking for food. She was following in the footsteps of Abraham, who taught us to welcome all guests.

*Bringing the Theme Closer*
- How do you prepare for a guest?
- What do you do when an invited guest comes to your home?

### *Being able to ask for help*

People in need came to Judith asking for help. When she needed help, she knew that King Solomon would help her.

*Bringing the Theme Closer*
- If you needed help, to whom would you go?
- What kind of help might you need?
- What kind of help could you give to someone else?

# CREATIVE FOLLOW-UP

## *Retelling the Story*

### Goals
To help the children understand the sequence of events in the story.
To help the children internalize the values in the story.

### IMPORTANT WORDS (3 AND 4-YEAR-OLDS)

**Description of Activity**
The children retell the story through the use of key words.

**Materials**
experience chart
felt markers

**Procedure**
1. Gather the children together in a circle.
2. Retell the story. While doing so, write key words or phrases on an experience chart.
3. Upon completion of the retelling, say a word or phrase, then choose a child to tell how that word or phrase fits into the story.
4. Continue this activity until everyone has had a turn or until interest wanes.

### LET'S PRETEND (5 AND 6-YEAR-OLDS)

**Description of Activity**
The children retell the story by role playing.

**Materials**
3 blocks (representing loaves of bread)
several brown paper bags (representing sacks of flour)
a box (representing an oven)
hats, jackets, a crown, and an apron (to serve as costumes for the characters)
a decorated large chair (representing a throne)
four scarves (to be waved by two children pretending to be the wind)

**Procedure**
1. After telling the story to the children, have half of the class act it out for the other half. Following this activity, the groups can change places and repeat the activity.
2. Distribute the following parts to volunteers:
   Judith
   each of Judith's visitors
   King Solomon
   the three sailors
   the wind (acted out by two children waving scarves and running past the sailors)
   a boat (5 children holding hands and forming an oval shape)
3. When everyone is ready to begin, retell the story. The actors can act their parts at the appropriate times.

## *Food Experiences*

**Goals**
To associate the preparation of *challah* with Shabbat.
To help the children understand the importance of sequencing in combining ingredients and baking the *challah*.

### BAKING CHALLAH (3 AND 4-YEAR-OLDS)

**Description of Activity**
Each child shapes the prepared dough to make a *challah*.

**Materials**
Ingredients for recipe below.

**Procedure**
1. Form a group of 4-6 children while the others are involved in free choice activities.
2. Instruct the participating children to wash their hands before the activity begins.
3. Make the *challah* according to the instructions below. While making the *challah*, introduce these questions:

What color is *challah* dough when it goes into the oven? What color is it when it is baked?

How big is a *challah* before it rises? After it rises? After it is baked?

## *Challah*

**Ingredients**
prepared dough (purchase at a kosher bakery or supermarket)
egg
sesame or poppy seeds
a few drops of water

**Supplies**
lightly greased baking sheets
1 small glass
1 pastry brush

**Method**
1. Help the children roll out the dough between their hands and then braid and twist it any way they wish.
2. The *challah* is then placed on the lightly greased baking sheet.
3. Break the egg into the glass. Examine it, and if it is satisfactory (no blood spots), it may be used.
4. Add a few drops of water to the egg and beat it well.
5. Using a pastry brush, spread the egg and water mixture over the *challah*.
6. Sprinkle the seeds on top and bake at 350 degrees for approximately one half hour.
7. Turn out immediately.

## BAKING CHALLAH (5 AND 6-YEAR-OLDS)

**Description of Activity**
The children make *challah* following the recipe below.

**Materials**
Ingredients for recipe below

**Procedure**
1. Make the *challah* according to the recipe below.

### *Rachel's Challah*
(Rachel Abramson, the author of this recipe, is Miriam Feinberg's niece)

**Ingredients**
3/4 cup sugar
2 cups lukewarm water
3/4 cup vegetable oil
1 tablespoon salt
5 small eggs
3 envelopes yeast
1/4 cup lukewarm water
10 cups flour
1 box raisins (if desired)

**Supplies**
2 large bowls
wax paper
several dish towels
lightly greased baking sheets
a pastry brush

**Method**
1. Combine first 4 ingredients in a large bowl.
2. Break the eggs into the glass and examine them to see if they are satisfactory. Add 4 of the eggs and mix together.
3. Mix yeast in 1/4 cup lukewarm water and add to other mixture.
4. Add 4 or 5 cups flour and beat well.
5. Gradually add 4 or 5 more cups flour.
6. Knead 8-10 minutes and place in a greased bowl.
7. Cover with wax paper and then with dish towel.
8. Let rise for one hour (until doubled).
9. Punch down and knead for a few minutes.
10. Let rise again until doubled (about 1/2 hour).
11. Knead down and divide into small round balls, giving each child a sufficient amount to work with.
12. Cover with dish towels and let rest for 10-15 minutes.
13. Raisins can be added here if desired. If so, they should be gently kneaded into the dough for a short period of time.
14. Mold and place the *challah* in a greased pan.
15. Break the remaining egg into the glass and examine it.

16. Add a few drops of water to the egg and beat well.
17. Using a pastry brush, spread the egg and water mixture over the *challah*.
18. Let the *challah* rise and brush again.
19. Sprinkle the seeds on top and bake at 350 degrees for 45-55 minutes.
20. Turn out immediately.

## *Baking and Breaking Bread Together*

### Goal
To teach the importance of bread to a meal.

To encourage the children to use safe and sanitary methods of food preparation.

## SANDWICH MAKING (3 AND 4-YEAR-OLDS)

### Description of Activity
The children make sandwiches to serve to homeless people in their community.

### Materials
loaves of white and whole wheat bread (enough for each child to make at least one sandwich)

peanut butter

jelly

several plastic knives

a box of plastic sandwich bags

a large paper bag

### Procedure
1. During free choice activity time, gather a small group of children together.
2. Explain that their task will be to make sandwiches for homeless people in their community.
3. After the children have washed their hands with soap and water, they make the sandwiches using the materials above.
4. After each sandwich has been made, place it into a sandwich bag. Place the filled bags into the large brown paper bag.

5. Repeat this activity with other small groups of children until everyone in the class has had an opportunity to participate.
6. Upon completion of the project, someone from a shelter for homeless people can come to the class, speak with the children about the shelter, and take the sandwiches to recipients.

## BAKING BREAD (5 AND 6-YEAR-OLDS)

### Description of Activity
The children bake bread, learn *HaMotzi*, and then make sandwiches to share with homeless people in their community.

### Materials
Ingredients for recipe below
peanut butter
jelly
several plastic knives
a box of plastic sandwich bags
a large paper bag

### Procedure
1. Gather together a small group of children during free choice activity time.
2. Instruct them to wash their hands with soap and water in preparation for baking bread.
3. After the group has been reassembled and the materials are made easily accessible, follow the procedure described below.

*Basic No-Knead Refrigerator Dough*
(Used with permission from *Recipes and Jewish Cooking Experiences For Pre-School Children* by Marcia R. Kargon, Baltimore Board of Jewish Education, 1983)

### Ingredients
1 envelope active dry yeast
2 tbs. warm water
2 tsp. salt
1/4 cup sugar
6 tbs. shortening

1 cup boiling water
1 egg, beaten well
3½ cups all purpose flour

**Supplies**
large mixing bowl
mixing spoon
measuring cups
measuring spoons
a water glass for examining the egg
waxed paper

**Procedure**
1. Soften the yeast in warm water.
2. Combine the salt, sugar, shortening and boiling water in a large mixing bowl. Cool to lukewarm.
3. Stir in the yeast, egg, and one cup of flour. Beat until smooth. continue adding flour, one cup at a time. Beat well after each addition. Cover and refrigerate overnight.
4. About 1½ hours before baking, turn out the dough onto a floured surface. Knead very slightly for a minute or so just to remove the air bubbles. Shape into rolls and place in greased baking and or muffin tins. Brush with oil or melted shortening. Allow dough to rise in a warm place about one hour until it doubles in bulk.
5. Bake in a pre-heated oven (425 degrees) for about 10 minutes or until browned.

## *Tasting Time*

### Goals
To create awareness of the variety of breads that exist.
To teach the children the blessings which are appropriate to recite before eating.

### LET'S TASTE (3 AND 4-YEAR-OLDS)

### Description of Activity
The children taste different kinds of breads.

## Materials
paper plates
napkins
a variety of breads such as:

| | |
|---|---|
| rye | white |
| pumpernickel | *challah* |
| whole wheat | cracked wheat |
| oatmeal | sourdough |

## Procedure
1. Gather the children together at circle time and discuss the variety of breads that exist.
2. Display a slice of each kind of bread discussed, noting the similarities and differences (color, texture, ingredients, etc.).
3. Then direct the children to wash their hands and gather at the snack tables.
4. Invite them to take one or more pieces of bread from the variety which have been placed on the snack tables.
5. Before eating, lead them in the following prayer:

   *Baruch Atah Adonai Eloheynu Melech Ha-olam Hamotzi Lechem Min Ha'aretz.*

   Blessed are You, Eternal our God, Ruler of the universe, Who brings forth bread from the earth.
6. At subsequent snack times, the children can bless and taste the other kinds of bread.

## LET'S TASTE (5 AND 6-YEAR-OLDS)

### Description of Activity
The children taste a variety of breads and learn about different grains.

### Materials
same as above
a variety of grains (obtain at a health food store)

**Procedure**
1. Gather the children together at circle time and discuss the variety of breads that exist.
2. Display a slice of each kind of bread discussed, noting the similarities and differences (color, texture, ingredients, etc.).
3. Then direct the children to wash their hands and gather at the snack tables.
4. Invite them to take one or more pieces of bread from the variety which have been placed on the snack tables.
5. Before eating, lead them in the following prayer:

*Baruch Atah Adonai Eloheynu Melech Ha-olam Hamotzi Lechem Min Ha'aretz.*

Blessed are You, Eternal our God, Ruler of the Universe, Who brings forth bread from the earth.

6. At a later time, gather together a small group of children.
7. Encourage them to handle the grains which are placed in close proximity. Discuss the grains, where they grow, where they were purchased, and what they look like when they are baked into bread.
8. With the help of the children, place each of the different kinds of grain into a small plastic bag. Attach the bag onto a poster board. Next to the bag, write the name of the grain and, if possible, attach a picture of the particular kind of bread made from that grain.

## TAKING THE STORY HOME

1. **Bread for the Homeless**
   Encourage the families to discuss ways that they can help the homeless, perhaps by baking or purchasing bread, making sandwiches, etc.

2. **Play a Game**
   Play the *Sack Blowing in the Wind* game. The first person in the family starts by saying, "I am the flour sack and when I was blowing in the wind, I saw . . . " Then the second person repeats what the first had said and adds, "Then this happened . . . " Continue the game until everyone has had a turn. (Very young children should not have to repeat the previous person's words if it is too difficult for them to do so. They can simply contribute their own ideas.)

3. **Story Starters**

Send home a list of story starters for the children to complete during carpool, at the dinner table, while taking a walk, etc.:

Every day Judith liked to . . .
A sad looking man came to Judith's door and told her that . . .
When Judith heard his story, she . . .
The next person who came to the door told Judith that . . .
The mother and child who came to the door said that . . .
When Judith discovered that her flour sack was empty she . . .
Three sailors told King Solomon that . . .

CHAPTER 10
# *The Treasure*

## BEFORE TELLING THE STORY

There is a feeling of satisfaction that people experience when they share with others in need. Even the poorest of people feel good when they share with those needier than they. Discuss this feeling with the children.

Treasures are items valued by their owners. Discuss treasures — what they might be, why people like them, and what people do with their treasures. Ask the children to tell the class about their own treasures or treasures owned by their families.

## TELLING THE STORY

There was once a kind and generous man named Abba Judah. He lived in the city of Antioch. Abba Judah had once been very rich. He used to give much of his money to help the poor. But then he, too, became poor. He had no money to share with others.

One day, Rabbi Joshua and some of his friends came to Antioch to collect money for poor students. Upon hearing about Rabbi Joshua's visit, Abba Judah felt sad.

"Why do you look so sad?" asked his wife.

"I'm embarrassed," answered Abba Judah. "I used to give money to the poor, but now that we're poor I have nothing to give. It makes me very sad."

"I have an idea," suggested his wife. "We still own a small field. Let's sell half of it and give the money we make on the sale to Rabbi Joshua. Then he can share it with the students."

Abba Judah loved the idea. "Of course!" he laughed. "A wonderful idea!"

He did just as his wife suggested. He sold part of his field and helped the poor students with the money which he was paid.

Some time later, while Abba Judah was plowing his field with the help of his plowing ox, the plow got caught on something in the ground. "Another large rock," thought Abba Judah. "Oh, my plow is broken. I won't be able to finish my work today. I'll have to get the plow fixed. Oh, no!"

# The Treasure

Abba Judah bent down and tried to remove a piece of the plow that broke off in the ground. He dug out some of the dirt around the plow blade. Then he dug out some more. "Hmmm," he thought, "there's something unusual here in the ground. It doesn't feel like a rock. It feels like a metal box."

Quickly, Abba Judah dug at the ground. Yes, it was a box. He took the box out of the ground and looked inside. He couldn't believe his eyes! It was a treasure.

First, Abba Judah took his ox to the stream where he might eat and drink. Once the ox was taken care of, Abba Judah picked up the box and started to walk. He walked faster and faster, and then he ran, and ran, and ran as fast as he could with the treasure box in his arms! He was so excited that he barely noticed how heavy it was.

"Oh, my!" he shouted to his wife. "Lucky us! Look what I found in our field! Oh, my! Oh, my!"

"Calm down, dear husband. Why are you so excited?" asked his wife, not knowing what to think about all the commotion. But when she saw the box and the treasure, she was very excited.

"Now we can buy a bigger field!" she shouted.

"Now, we can buy a new plow," Abba Judah laughed. And they both laughed and hugged.

Abba Judah and his wife used the treasure to buy a bigger field. They were very happy that they could now grow enough crops to feed themselves, but they were happiest of all that once again they had money to share with the poor.

**Questions on the Story**
1. Why did Abba Judah feel sad?
2. Do you think his wife's suggestion was a good one? Why or why not?
3. What happened to Abba Judah's plow? What caused this to happen?
4. What did Abba Judah do first when he found the treasure?
5. What did Abba Judah and his wife do with the treasure?
6. What is a treasure?

## THEMES IN THE STORY

*Giving to the poor*
   Abba Judah and his wife were always concerned about caring for the poor.

*Bringing the Theme Closer*
- Why do you think that there are food and clothing collection boxes in public places?
- Have you ever seen a *tzedakah* box at home, in a friend's home, or in school? What goes in the *tzedakah* box? How do we use the contents of the box?

*The value of sharing with others*
   Abba Judah's wife wanted to sell half of their small field and share the money with poor students. Then they would be able to help the students and still have a small field for growing crops.

*Bringing the Theme Closer*
- What does sharing mean?
- Have you ever shared something with someone else? What was it? Why did you share it? How did you feel when you shared? How did the other person feel?

## CREATIVE FOLLOW-UP

### Retelling the Story

#### Goals
   To help the children sequence the events of the story.
   To help the children understand the events in the story.

### HATS (3 AND 4-YEAR-OLDS)

#### Description of Activity
   The children learn the events of the story by "telling it" through the use of hats.

**Materials**
　　construction paper in a variety of colors
　　scraps of construction paper in a variety of colors
　　one pair of scissors
　　white glue
　　stapler

**Procedure**
1. Before meeting with the children, prepare hats using the materials above and the diagram and instructions below:

### *Abba Judah's Hat*
a. Cut three strips of construction paper 2" inches wide and 18" long.

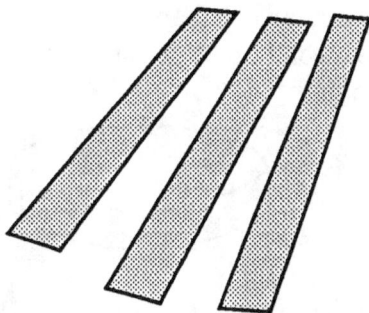

b. Bring the ends of one of the strips together and glue them so that they make a circular headband.

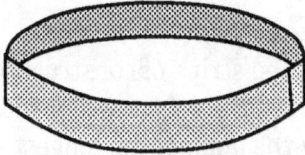

c. Glue the ends of the second strip to the headband so that one end is in the front and the other in the back.

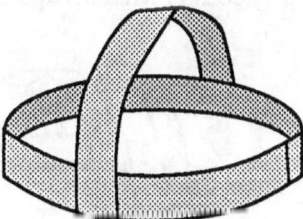

d. Glue the ends of the third strip to either side of the headband so that it cuts across the middle.

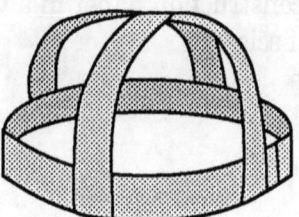

### Abba Judah's Wife's Hat
a. Cut three strips of construction paper 2" inches wide and 18" long.
b. Bring the ends of one of the strips together and glue them so that they make a circular headband.
c. Glue the second and third strips to the sides of the headband to resemble hair.

### Rabbi Joshua's Hat
a. Cut three strips of construction paper, one of them 2" wide and 18" long, and the other two 2" wide and 10" long.
b. Bring the ends of the longest strip together and glue them so that they make a circular headband.
c. Stretch each of the two remaining strips across the headband, folding down and gluing the ends of those strips to the headband.
d. Decorate the hat with scraps of construction paper in a variety of colors.

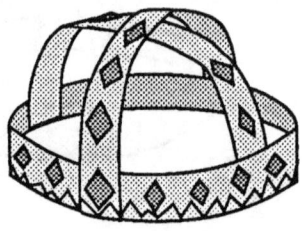

## The Ox's Hat

    a. Cut one strip of construction paper 2" wide and 18" long.

    b. Glue the overlapping ends of the strip together so that it makes a head band.

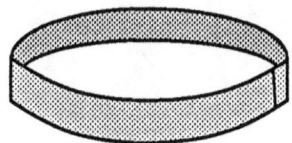

    c. Cut two 4" triangles.

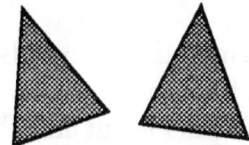

    d. Glue the triangles to the headband, approximately 6" apart.

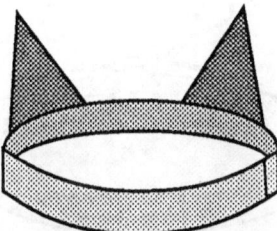

2. Bring the children together at circle time and retell the story.
3. As reference to a particular character is made, hand a hat to a child.
4. Continue telling the story while encouraging the child to act out the part of the character whose hat he/she is wearing.
5. When the activity is finished, place the hats back in their boxes and place the boxes in a designated dress-up area. Encourage the children to use the hats during play on subsequent days.

## HATS (5 AND 6-YEAR-OLDS)

### Description of Activity

The children learn the events of the story by retelling it through the use of hats.

**Materials**
paper plates (3 per each child)
construction paper
scissors
stapler
white glue
yarn
pieces of felt

**Procedure**
1. Gather a small group of children together and review the story with them.
2. Discuss the different characters in the story and encourage the children to describe them.
3. Place all of the materials in an easily accessible area and describe how a simple hat can be made.
4. Encourage each child to cut out a big circle in the center of a paper plate. Be sure that the plate rim fits on the child's head securely. The children might need some assistance with this task.

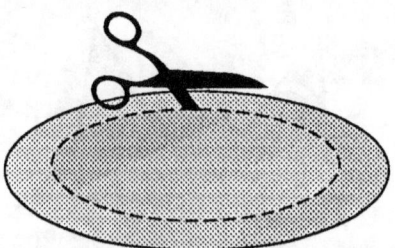

5. Encourage the children to decorate their hats as they imagine the hat of a particular character in the story looked.
6. Repeat this activity until every child has created a hat.
7. The children can then meet in a large group and act out the story while the teacher narrates it. All of the Abba Judahs should wear their hats and act as they think Abba Judah did, all of the wives should wear their hats and act as they think Abba Judah's wife did, etc.
8. When the activity is finished, store the hats in boxes and place the boxes in the dress-up area. Encourage children to incorporate the hats in their play.

## Art Activity

### Goal
To help the children understand what a treasure is, and why it is kept in a special place.

### MAKE A TREASURE BOX (3 AND 4-YEAR-OLDS)

#### Description of Activity
The children create a treasure box with an assortment of materials.

#### Materials
a very big box with a lid (from a large electrical appliance)
shiny wallpaper, cut up into pieces
aluminum foil, cut into pieces
yarn, cut in a variety of lengths
ribbons
white glue

#### Procedure

1. Gather a small group of children together around a table with the materials above within easy reach.
2. Discuss a treasure box — its appearance, its use, and items that might be found in it.
3. Encourage the children to decorate the box with the materials provided so that it looks the way they think a treasure box might look.
4. On subsequent days, other groups of children may add to the decorations until all of the children have been given the opportunity to decorate the box.
5. After everyone has had a turn decorating the box, place it in a prominent place in the classroom.

### MAKE A TREASURE BOX (5 AND 6-YEAR-OLDS)

#### Description of Activity
The children make a treasure box and decorate it with items collected on a nature walk.

### Materials
items collected on a nature walk (leaves, twigs, stones, etc.)
items brought from home (buttons, pieces of fabric, remnants of wallpaper, etc.)
items found in the building (colored paper, etc.)

### Procedure
1. Review the story with the children.
2. Discuss treasure boxes — their appearance, their use, and the items that might be found in them.
3. Ask the children to bring items from home that they think can be used for decorations.
4. On another day, take the children on a walk outdoors to choose items that can be used in decorating the box.
5. On still another day, take the children on a walk in the building. Stop in at an office and inquire if there are scraps which can be donated to the art project.
6. Bring all of the assorted materials together and display them on a table so that they are easily accessible.
7. Encourage the children to use all the materials they gathered to decorate the box so that it looks the way they think a treasure box might look.
8. On subsequent days, encourage other groups of children to add to the decorations on the box until all of the children have had a turn.
9. Upon completion of the project, place the box in a prominent place in the classroom.

## *Preparing Gifts*

### Goals
To help the children develop a sense of concern for those in need.
To help the children understand that there are many ways to help the needy, including giving money.

### A TREASURE GIFT (3 AND 4-YEAR-OLDS)

### Description of Activity
The children bring gifts from home and create a large greeting card to give to needy youngsters.

### Materials
    appropriate gifts for needy children, such as crayons, felt markers, story books, toys, etc.
    construction paper
    felt markers
    crayons
    treasure box made by this group in previous activity

### Procedure
1. Discuss with the children the *mitzvah* of concern for the poor and needy.
2. Try to help the children think of various ways of helping the needy.
3. Ask them to bring something to school during the next few days to give to needy children their age.
4. Send home a note to the parents describing this activity, its purpose, and procedure.
5. As the gifts are brought to school, place them in the treasure box.
6. Help the children to design a large greeting card with construction paper. Write down the children's greetings to the recipient as they are dictated.
7. Gather small groups of children together until all of them have had a chance to participate and the card is completed.
8. When the greeting card is completed, invite a representative of the recipient organization to visit the classroom and talk with the children. The children can help the representative to carry the treasures to her/his car.

## TREASURE HUNT (5 AND 6-YEAR-OLDS)

### Description of Activity
    The children bring gifts to school to give to needy youngsters. Then they hide the gifts, search for them, and place them in a treasure box.

### Materials
    appropriate gifts for needy children (crayons, felt markers, books, toys, etc.)
    construction paper
    felt markers
    crayons
    treasure box made by this group in previous activity

**Procedure**
1. Discuss the *mitzvah* of concern for the poor and needy.
2. Help the children think of various ways of helping the needy.
3. Ask the children to bring something to school during the next few days to give to needy children their age.
4. Send home a note to the parents describing this activity, its purpose, and procedure.
5. Hide the gifts the children bring in for the needy around the classroom. Include a few additional ones in case some children have forgotten to bring something.
6. Gather the children together and describe a treasure hunt.
7. Children then hunt around the room for a gift. All found gifts are placed in the treasure box.
8. The children come back to the circle and take turns describing the gifts they found.
9. Help the children to design a large greeting card with construction paper. Write down the children's greetings to the recipient as they are dictated.
10. Gather small groups of children together until all of them have had a chance to participate, and the card is completed.

## *Displaying and Storing Treasures*

### Goals
To help the children understand the importance of a proper place to display and store treasures.
To help the children realize that treasures reflect each person's individuality.

### TREASURE COLLAGE (3 AND 4-YEAR-OLDS)

**Description of Activity**
The children design collages with their treasures.

**Materials**
one cardboard or styrofoam tray for each child
one cup salt
one cup warm water
2 tsp. salad oil

a small sack of flour
a large bowl
a mixing spoon

### Procedure
1. In advance, send home a note to parents requesting that children bring in a treasure on a specific day.
2. Mix together in the bowl, the salt, warm water, oil, and enough flour to make a sticky "goop."
3. Around a table, gather together a small group of children with the treasures they have brought from home.
4. Give each child a tray. Make the goop easily accessible.
5. Help each child to place a handful of goop on the tray.
6. Then each child can place his/her treasures in the goop.
7. Place the tray in a place where it can dry.
8. After the goop has dried, the children can take their treasure collages home or keep them on display in school.

## MUSEUM OF TREASURES (5 AND 6-YEAR-OLDS)

### Description of Activity
The children create display cases for their museum, then display their personal treasures in the class museum.

### Materials
9 boxes without lids (the size of shoe boxes or bigger)
masking tape
tempera paint (in various colors)
4 paint brushes
several sheets of newspapers
the children's personal treasures
index cards
felt markers

### Procedure
1. After retelling the story, gather a small group of children together during free choice activity time. Discuss treasures, and ways to display them for others to see and appreciate. Talk about museums. Consider the ways that

treasures are displayed in museums so that visitors can see and appreciate them.
2. Place all the materials on a table covered by newspapers.
3. Encourage the children to paint the boxes inside and out in imaginative ways.
4. After the group has painted for a while, encourage them to exchange places with some of the other children. Repeat this activity until all of the children have had an opportunity to paint.
5. After the paint has thoroughly dried, arrange the boxes so that they create a pyramid with the openings facing forward.

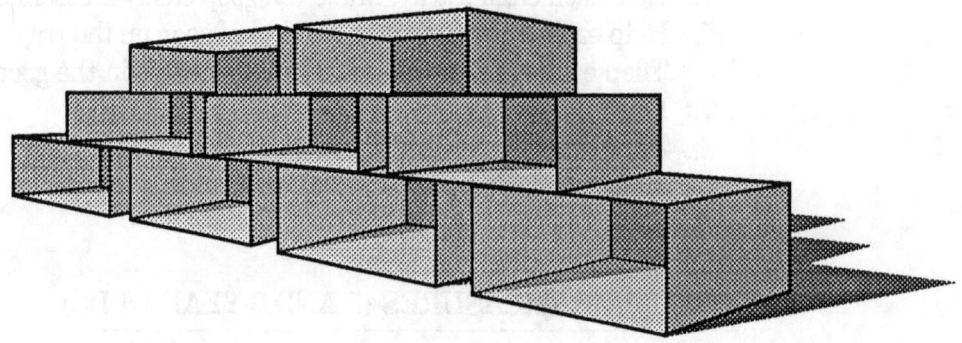

6. Have the children secure the boxes together with masking tape.
7. Encourage the children to bring their treasures to school for display in the "Museum of Treasures." The children should write their names on index cards and place the cards next to their treasures.

## TAKING THE STORY HOME

1. **Adopt a Charity**
   Suggest to parents that they adopt and support a charity. Children can more easily relate to a local charity than one that is far away. Suggestions for gifts are: outgrown clothing; used toys in good condition; used children's books in good condition; toys, children's books, and canned goods purchased with money which has been contributed by family members.

2. **Story Starters**
   Send home a list of story starters for the children to complete during carpool, at the dinner table, while taking a walk, etc.:

When Abba Judah was rich he...
Rabbi Joshua wanted to collect money so that...
Abba Judah was sad because...
Abba Judah's wife suggested that...
One day when Abba Judah was plowing his field...
Abba Judah decided to use the treasure money for...

3. **Family Treasure Box**

    Suggest to parents that they create a family treasure box for items that will become family heirlooms. Make the box as follows:

    **Materials**

    a sturdy box (shoe box, cigar box, etc.)
    ribbon
    fabric
    lace
    beads
    buttons
    sequins
    yarn
    scissors
    white glue

    **Procedure**
    1. Glue any of the materials listed above onto the box, in any design preferred.
    2. Let the box dry completely before storing treasures in it.
    3. Here are a few suggestions for items to store in the family treasure box: selected drawings created by the children; photographs of each family member (as well as of the entire family) taken at special occasions (birthdays, holiday celebrations, family vacations, etc.); special jewelry; audiotapes containing conversations and songs made by individual family members.

CHAPTER 11
# *Honest Scales*

## BEFORE TELLING THE STORY

Lead a classroom discussion on the importance of rain to those who live on farms and grow crops, and also to those who live in cities and towns and buy food that came from the farms. Ask the children to suggest some ideas for coping without rainfall.

Discuss measuring — what we measure, why we measure, and what we use as measuring implements. Mention measuring devices, such as scales, rulers, cups, spoons, and any others suggested by the children.

## TELLING THE STORY

A group of people came to see the Rabbi of a small town. "Rabbi," they said, "please help us. You know it has not rained for a long, long, long time. The farmers don't have enough water for their fields. Because of this, the crops are not growing. The people don't have enough to eat. What should we do?"

"I will pray for God's help," promised the Rabbi. "Maybe my prayers will be answered and it will soon rain. In the meantime, let us hope that everyone will give *tzedakah* to help those who need it."

In his sleep that night, the Rabbi had a dream. In his dream, he heard a voice. "Only one man in this town can help," the voice said. "That man is Kalman, the grocer. Tell all the people in the town to come to the synagogue and pray. Kalman will lead the prayers."

When the Rabbi woke up, he thought, "What a strange dream. Kalman cannot read well. Sometimes he's not so nice to the customers who come to his store. I wonder why he would be chosen to lead the prayers. Oh, well, it was only a dream. I don't have to pay attention to it."

That day, the Rabbi went to the synagogue. He lead the people in prayer. He talked to them. He helped them. He did all the things that Rabbis do. But, it did not rain.

That next night, the Rabbi had another dream. Again a voice spoke to him. "Remember, only one man in this town can help. You must call Kalman the grocer to come and lead the prayers in the synagogue."

When the Rabbi awoke, he thought about his dream. "This time I will call all the people to the synagogue," he thought. "I will send messengers to tell every man, woman, and child to come to the synagogue right away."

The people of the town hurried to the synagogue. At first, there were ten people there. Then there were 32 people. Then there were 87 people. And then, before long . . . the Rabbi was really amazed . . . there were 258 people! Almost all of the people of the village were there — men, women, children, even babies! And they were all talking at once. "What's happening?" "Why did the Rabbi call us together?" "Is everything all right?" They asked each other one question after another.

The 259th person to come to the synagogue was Kalman the grocer. He was the very last person to arrive.

"Kalman," the Rabbi called out in a big booming voice. Everyone turned to stare at Kalman. "What had he done?" they wondered. Kalman wondered, too.

"Please lead us in prayer today," said the Rabbi sweetly.

"Why me, Rabbi?" asked Kalman, and he started to perspire from nervousness. "I don't know how to read well, Rabbi."

"It doesn't matter, dear Kalman," said the Rabbi. "Read the prayers you know. Please, just as a special favor to me."

Now Kalman was shaking, he was that nervous. He took off his *tallit*, put it on his seat, and walked out of the synagogue.

No one had ever done that before!

No one in the synagogue said a word! No one in the synagogue moved! The Rabbi stood still. All the people stood still. One minute passed. Five minutes passed. Fifteen minutes passed.

Suddenly, the squeaky synagogue door opened. All heads turned toward the back of the synagogue. There stood Kalman, holding the scales he used each day to weigh flour in his store. Without saying a word, he walked to the *bimah*. Everyone watched. No one spoke.

Kalman lifted his scales up as high as he could. "God," he called in a tiny, weak voice. "I am not a learned man. I cannot read well. I have worked hard all of my life. Sometimes I have been impatient with my customers. But I have always been honest. I have kept these scales clean and straight and I was never unfair to anyone. If you believe me, God, I pray that this drought should end, and that the rain should start, so that the crops will grow, and your people will have food to eat."

Then Kalman lowered his scales. He was very still and very quiet. The Rabbi was quiet. All the men, the women, the children, and even the babies were quiet.

Suddenly, a soft wind gusted against the windows. The sky grew dark. Everyone strained to listen. "Drip, drip, drip." At first it was slow and quiet. Then it got louder, "DRip, DRip, DRip," and louder still, "DROP, PLOP, POUR!"

"It's raining! It's raining!" screamed the people. "The town is saved!" Everyone hugged and kissed and danced and sang and laughed.

All the people were so happy with the rain, they didn't even mind walking home in it. It rained and rained until there was enough water for the crops. Then it stopped raining, and everyone came out of their houses to look at how beautiful their town and their fields and their trees and flowers and crops were.

When the Rabbi went out to admire his beautiful town, there was a line of people waiting to see him. "Rabbi," each one said. "I didn't realize how important it was for me to check the scales in my store to make sure they were working well. After Kalman prayed for our town, I went to my store and found out that my scale was not adjusted. My customers were not getting a fair measure. So I fixed the scales right away. I want to be as honest as I can."

One by one, each of the town's storekeepers came to tell their story to the Rabbi.

Then the Rabbi ordered that a painting of the scales of Kalman the grocer be placed in the hall of the synagogue. He wanted every person to know how important it is to have honest scales. Everyone was very proud that Kalman lived in their town and that he helped to teach them about the importance of having honest scales.

## Questions on the Story
1. Why did the people of the town visit the Rabbi when they had a problem?
2. Why do you think the Rabbi had the same dream twice?
3. Why did the Rabbi tell all the people to come to the synagogue?
4. What was special about Kalman?
5. What did Kalman teach everyone?
6. Why was a painting of Kalman's scales kept in the synagogue lobby?

# THEMES IN THE STORY

### *All living things need rain*
The people in the town worried that the crops would die without rain.

*Bringing the Theme Closer*
- Can you name some plants that would die without rain?
- Do you have some plants in your home or classroom that need to be watered? How often are they watered? Who waters them?

### *People should be honest in their dealings with others*
Kalman reminded everyone in the town about the importance of being honest in their dealings with others.

*Bringing the Theme Closer*
- Can you think of some times when you were honest with your friends or family? Give an example of such a time.
- Can you think of a time when someone told you something that you thought was not true?

# CREATIVE FOLLOW-UP

## *Retelling The Story*

### Goals
To help the children understand the sequence of events in the story.
To encourage the children to describe the feelings of the people in the story.

## STORY PICTURES (3 AND 4-YEAR-OLDS)

### Description of Activity
The children express through drawings the feelings described in the story.

### Materials
construction or drawing paper
pencils
crayons

### Procedure
1. Following the telling of the story, and during free choice activity time, gather 3 or 4 children together.
2. Invite them to discuss their favorite parts of the story.
3. Make the materials easily accessible and encourage the children to draw a picture of their favorite parts of the story.
4. Ask them to dictate while you write their words on their papers.

## WORD PICTURES (5 AND 6-YEAR-OLDS)

### Description of Activity
The children retell the events of the story by talking into a tape recorder.

### Materials
tape-recorder

### Procedure
1. After telling the story, gather the children together at circle time.
2. Assign different characters of the story to the children. There can be a role for everyone since some of the children can serve as members of the congregation.
3. Interview each of the characters in the story, encouraging them to speak their parts into the tape recorder.
4. Upon completion of the tape, play it for the children. Then place it in the listening center with a tape recorder for use during free choice activity time.

## *Ways To Measure*

### Goal
To provide opportunities for the children to practice using various forms of measurement.

### COUNTING OBJECTS (3 AND 4-YEAR-OLDS)

#### Description of Activity
The children count the number of objects inside a plastic container.

#### Materials
several identical empty plastic containers with tops (yogurt or L'Eggs hosiery containers)
several pennies

#### Procedure
1. Gather a small group of children together during free choice activity time.
2. After placing some of the objects into each of the containers, put the tops back on.
3. Move the containers around so that it is not clear how many pennies are in each container.
4. Encourage each of the children to pick up a container, shake it, and guess how many pennies are inside.
5. After they guess the number of objects inside the containers, suggest that they open the containers, empty the pennies and count them.
6. Repeat this activity with additional groups of children until all of them have had an opportunity to participate.

### PITCHERS OF WATER (5 AND 6-YEAR-OLDS)

#### Description of Activity
The children pour different amounts of water into each of 8-10 glasses. They then place them in order from the least to the most amount of water per glass.

**Materials**
    8-10 drinking glasses of identical sizes
    several pitchers
    water

**Procedure**
1. Gather a small group of children together. Suggest that they pour water from the pitchers into the glasses.
2. Encourage them to place the glasses in order depending upon the amount of water in each glass.
3. Then suggest that they mix up the order of the glasses or pour more water into some of them and reorder them.
4. This activity should be repeated with other small groups of children, giving all of the children an opportunity to participate. Children can do this again later during free choice activity time.

## *Experimenting*

**Goal**
To help the children understand why it rains.

### MAKING RAIN (3 AND 4-YEAR-OLDS)

**Description of Activity**
The children observe boiling water as it condenses like falling rain.

**Materials**
    a saucepan with a lid
    water

**Procedure**
1. Gather a small group of children together.
2. Talk about rain — how the sky looks just before it rains, how rain feels, what rain does to the soil, and how rain helps things grow.
3. Fill the saucepan halfway with water and place it on a stove burner or hot plate.
4. After assuring that the children are at a safe distance from the saucepan, bring the water to a boil.

5. As the water boils, remove the lid, holding it above the saucepan.
6. Note that as more and more steam covers the lid, tiny drops of water form and then fall back into the pan.
7. Ask the children to describe their observations.

> **Making Rain**
> 1. Sara said, "There were bubbles when the water got hotter."
> 2. Danny saw drops of water on the lid of the pot.
> 3. Ezra saw steam coming out of the pot.

## RAIN CYCLE (5 AND 6-YEAR-OLDS)

### Description of Activity
The children learn about the condensation of moisture and the formation of rain by observing the interaction of moisture, warm air, and cold air.

### Materials
2 large self-sealing plastic bags
masking tape
1/2 cup water
a few ice cubes

### Procedure
1. On a sunny day, after retelling the story, gather the children together and discuss rain and what the weather looks and feels like just prior to rainfall.
2. Seal all the seams at the bottom of the plastic bag with masking tape.
3. Pour 1/2 cup of water into the plastic bag, taking care to keep the water from touching the sides of the bag.
4. Discuss the purpose of this activity with the children: Through the use of this water, which is like a puddle, they will find out where the water goes when it dries up.

5. Gather together the top of the bag and seal it. Tape it onto a window in the warmest, sunniest place in the room, where it is easily visible to all.

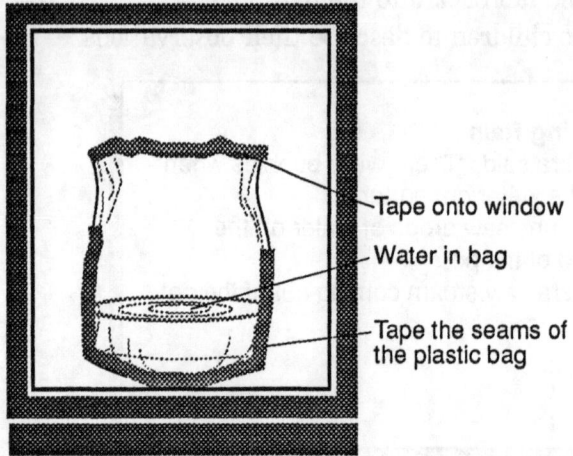

6. Point out to the children that the top of the bag is dry and all of the water is at the bottom.
7. After a few hours, gather the children together and draw their attention to the bag.
8. Feel the water. It should feel warmer than it did a few hours previously.
9. Encourage the children to observe the upper part of the bag and describe their observations. Condensation should have appeared there. Clouds contain tiny drops of water like those that can be seen on the inside of the bag.
10. Place the ice cubes in a second plastic bag and seal the bag.
11. Either tape the bag of ice cubes onto the window or hold it there, overlapping the bag of water.

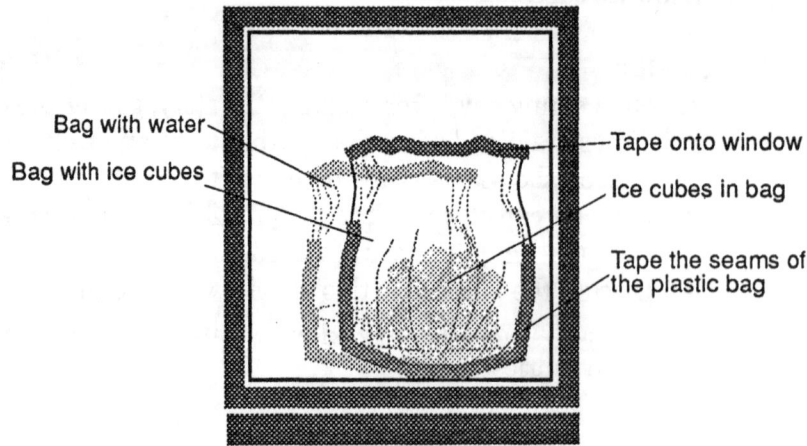

12. Observe that the water in the first bag condenses and drips down into the puddle below. As with rain, the ice in the second bag acts as cool air high in the sky causing the rain drops to fall.

# TAKING THE STORY HOME

## 1. Story Starters

Send home a list of story starters for the children to complete during carpool, at the dinner table, while taking a walk, etc.:

People in the town were worried when it hadn't rained for a long time because...

One night while the Rabbi slept, he...

In his dream there was...

All the people came to the synagogue and...

When Kalman came to the synagogue, he...

Some of the other storekeepers told the Rabbi that...

## 2. Conserving Water

Encourage parents to talk with their children about conserving water. They can then make a chart on which it will be noted what each person plans to do to conserve water at home, in school, at work, or while with friends. Magazine pictures or sketches can be pasted on the chart to describe each person's contribution as shown below.

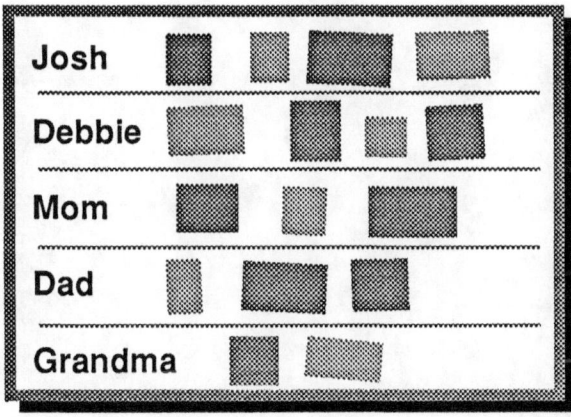

3. **Family Scrapbook**
   Suggest to parents that each family member collect articles and pictures from newspapers and magazines about rain, drought, and water problems. Paste each of these items in the scrapbook while discussing the importance of water to all of life, and ways in which to encourage water conservation.

CHAPTER 12

# *Little Becomes Much*

## BEFORE TELLING THE STORY

Read *The Carrot Seed* by Ruth Kraus. Discuss ways to encourage crops to grow (providing sun, water, earth, loving care, etc.).

Discuss the responsibilities that a person must take upon himself/herself when agreeing to take care of other people's things.

## TELLING THE STORY

Rabbi Pinhas Ben Yair was a very good man. He was always kind, and he especially liked to help poor people.

One day he heard a knock, knock, knock at the door. When he opened it, he found two men who were wearing old torn clothing. One was dressed in blue and the other in gray. They did not seem happy.

"Please come in," the Rabbi said with a welcoming smile. "How I can help you."

Each of the poor, sad men was carrying a small sack. The man in the blue robe said, "Rabbi Pinhas, we need to ask you for a favor. Could we leave these sacks with you? In each sack there is grain. It's very good grain, but we can't plant it at this time. We have been having a hard time supporting our families and we need to find work somewhere else. When things are better, we'll come back for the grain."

"Of course, of course. No problem," laughed Rabbi Pinhas. "And why not?"

"Oh, thank you so very much. We'll keep in touch with you," said the men. They left the Rabbi's house and went on their way.

Rabbi Pinhas put the little sacks of grain in a cool dark place. He would keep the grain safe until the men returned.

A week went by. The two men did not come back for their sacks. A month passed. The men did not return. Several months passed and still the men did not return.

"I must do something with this grain," thought Rabbi Pinchas. "If not, it will get spoiled and no one will be able to use it."

So he went out to his field. He cleared away the rocks and big stones. He plowed the soil. And when the ground was ready, he planted the grain.

"Whew! Now I feel much better," he said. "The grain won't spoil if it is planted in the ground."

Rabbi Pinhas took very good care of the grain that he had planted. He watered it, he weeded the field, and he watched the grain grow. Before long, he had a field of tall stalks of wheat. So, he harvested the wheat. Then he put the harvested wheat into a grain bin called a silo so that it would not spoil. Still the men did not return.

Soon it was planting season again. Rabbi Pinchas took some of the grain in the silo back out to his fields. He plowed and planted and watered and weeded just as he had done before. Then he waited and watched as this new crop of wheat grew tall. When the wheat was ready, he harvested it and filled the silo with more harvested wheat. And so the years passed. Rabbi Pinchas kept planting and harvesting, planting and harvesting, planting and harvesting. He worked very hard year after year for seven years. The silo was filled to the very top with grain.

Rabbi Pinhas stood back and looked at his full silo. He felt good about all the work he had done to fill up that huge silo during those years.

One day, two men came to Rabbi Pinhas' house and knocked at the door.

When Rabbi Pinhas opened his door, he noticed something familiar about those men. One wore a gray garment and the other a blue one. They looked tired and sad. He knew that he had seen them somewhere before. But where?

"We have come to collect the two small sacks of grain that we left with you seven years ago," said the one in blue.

"Well, what do you know?" laughed Rabbi Pinhas. "I'm certainly happy to see you at last. Unfortunately, you won't be able to carry the grain by yourselves."

"What do you mean?" asked the one in gray, a puzzled look on his face. "You promised you would take care of our grain. Did you lose the sacks? Did you sell them? Did someone steal them? Where are they?"

"Now that's an interesting story," smiled Rabbi Pinhas. "You see, when you left the two small sacks here and didn't come back for them, I worried that the grain would spoil. So I decided to plant it. After I planted it, it needed to be harvested. After the harvest, it needed to be stored. And then, as the seasons passed, some of it had to be planted all over again. I did this year after year for seven years. Would you like to see what your two small sacks of grain look like now?"

Rabbi Pinhas took his two visitors to see his silo. "Our small sacks of grain have grown until they fill a silo!" laughed the one in gray. "Who would ever have thought this would happen to us?" And the two sad men turned into two smiling, laughing, happy men. They jumped, and danced, and hugged each other. "We're rich! We're rich!" they shouted.

The men went to get donkeys and camels so that they could carry their grain back home. They filled bag after bag. They loaded donkey after donkey and camel after camel. Fill, fill, fill and load, load, load was what they did for a whole day. At the end of the day, they were tired but happy. Suddenly, as they were about to leave, the one in blue turned to his friend and said, "I can't believe it!"

"Tell me. What?" said the other.

"We're taking all of the grain. We didn't offer to share it with Rabbi Pinhas. And without his help we wouldn't have this grain."

"Oh, my! You're right! And besides sharing it with Rabbi Pinhas, maybe we should share it with some people who don't have enough to eat."

So the two men unloaded some of the sacks of grain and gave them to Rabbi Pinhas. Then they unloaded some more sacks of grain and asked Rabbi Pinhas to share them with those in need.

And, of course, Rabbi Pinhas was happy to do that because helping others was one of his most favorite things to do. Then off the men went with their donkeys and camels loaded with grain. And the faces of both men were loaded with smiles.

### Questions on the Story
1. Why did the two men knock on Rabbi Pinhas Ben Yair's door?
2. What did they ask him to do?
3. What did Rabbi Pinhas do with the grain?
4. Why did he do that?

5. What did the two poor men find when they came back after seven years?
6. Were they surprised? Were you surprised?

## THEMES IN THE STORY

### *Returning property to its rightful owner*
Rabbi Pinhas Ben Yair was concerned about making sure that the grain would be returned to its rightful owner.

*Bringing the Theme Closer*
- Had someone ever asked you to watch something for him/her? What was it? How did you take care of it? Did you give it back in good condition?
- Did someone ever take care of your things? Were you happy with the way he/she took care of them?

### *Keeping a promise*
Rabbi Pinhas kept his promise to the men who left the grain with him.

*Bringing the Theme Closer*
- What is a promise?
- Have you ever made a promise? What was it?
- Was it hard or easy for you to keep the promise?

### *Not wasting*
Rabbi Pinhas did not waste any of the grain; nor did he allow it to spoil.

*Bringing the Theme Closer*
- What can you do so as not to waste food?
- Do you save bottles, cans, or newspaper for recycling in your neighborhood?

## CREATIVE FOLLOW UP

### *Retelling the Story*

**Goal**

To help the children sequence the events in the story.

## PAPER BAG ROBES (3 AND 4-YEAR-OLDS)

### Description of Activity
The children create costumes, then dress up in them to retell the story.

### Materials
large paper grocery bags (at least one per child)
several pairs of scissors
felt markers
white glue
pieces of yarn
buttons
sparkles
sequins

### Procedure
1. In advance of this activity, ask each child to bring a large paper grocery bag to school.
2. Place the materials listed above on a work table. Then tell the story.
3. Invite a small group to the table.
3. Discuss the story and encourage children to create costumes for use when acting it out. Help them to decide which story character they would like to pretend to be.
4. Turn each paper bag upside down and cut out arm holes on the sides and a hole for the head on the top. Cut straight up the front of the bag from bottom to top, creating an opening in the "robe" as is shown in the illustration below.

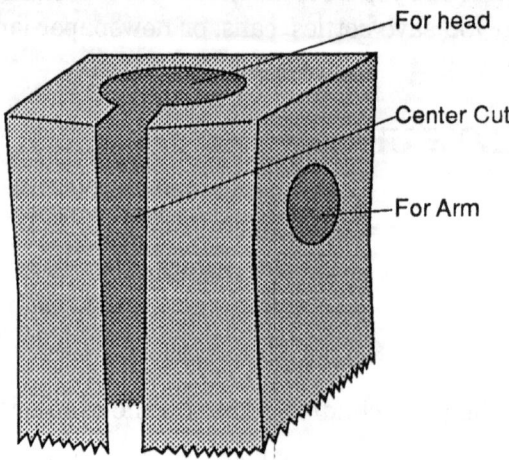

5. Encourage the children to decorate their bags as they wish using the materials listed above.
6. When this group completes this task, invite another small group to make costumes. Continue until all of the children have had an opportunity to create their costumes.
7. When all of the children have made their costumes, retell the story. Each child can act out his/her part as the story is told.

## YARN PEOPLE (5 AND 6-YEAR-OLDS)

### Description of Activity
Children make yarn people to represent characters in the story. They use these to retell the story.

### Materials
several pieces of cardboard (some 12" and some 6" in length)
several pairs of scissors
several balls of yarn in a variety of colors

### Procedure
1. Following the telling of the story, gather together 3 or 4 children during free choice activity time.
2. Place the materials in an easily accessible location. Explain to the children that you will help them create "yarn people" representing story characters.
3. Each child starts by winding yarn around a 12" long piece of cardboard 24 times.

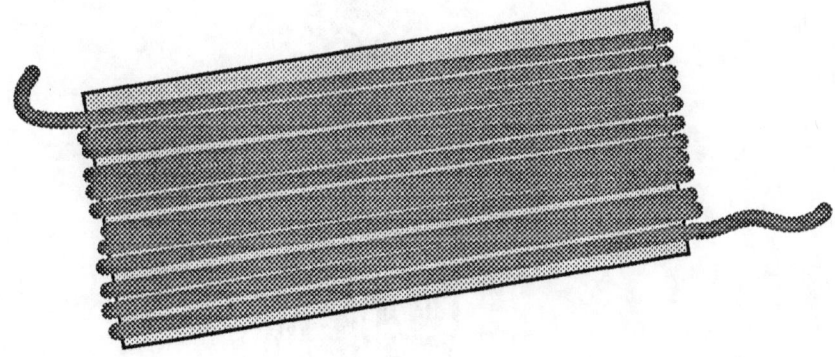

4. Slip the yarn off the cardboard. Using another piece of yarn, tie the yarn person in two places, one about 1/2" from an end and another about 3/4" from that same end. This makes the head and the body of the yarn person.

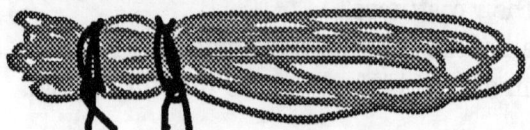

5. The children now wind yarn around a 6" piece of cardboard 12 times.

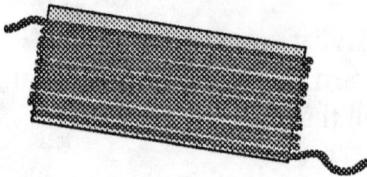

6. Slip that yarn off the cardboard and tie it with another piece of yarn in two places, each about 3/4" from the end. Now the arms and hands have been created.

7. Slip the arms and hands yarn through the body yarn right below the place that was tied for the head.

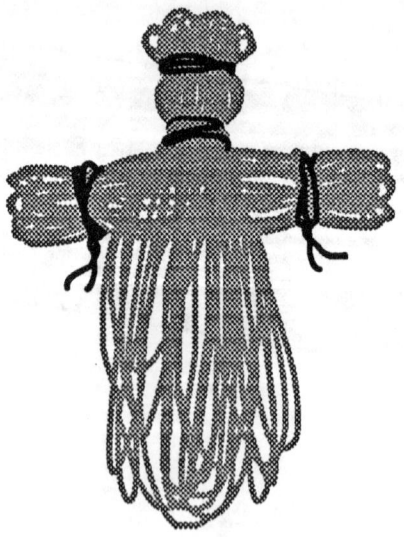

8. Using a new piece of yarn, now tie the waist of the body just below the arms.

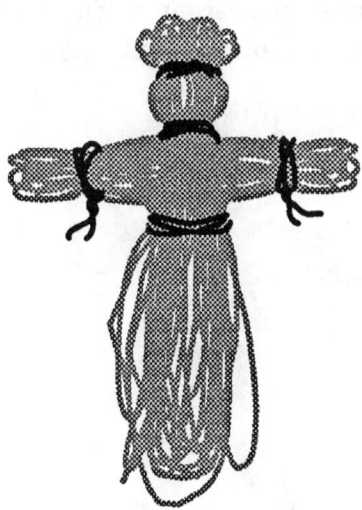

9. If desired, cut the top loops of the head to look like hair.

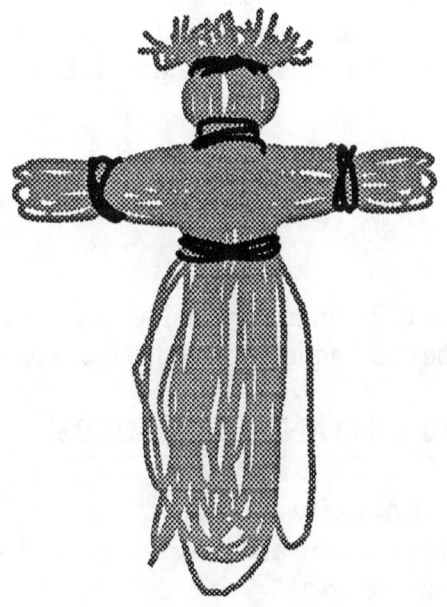

10. For a yarn person wearing a dress, leave as is. For one representing one of the men in the story, tie another piece of yarn about an inch below the waist. Divide the yarn in half at the bottom for legs. Tie each leg with a piece of yarn about 1/2" from the end.

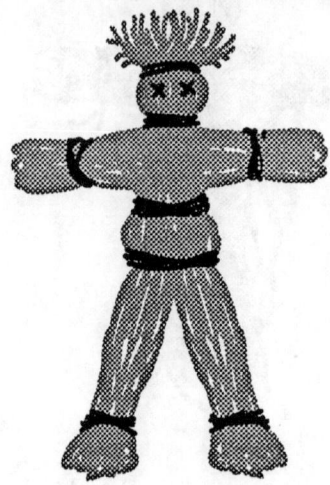

11. After the yarn people are completed, retell the story. The children can use their yarn people to represent particular characters at the appropriate times as the story is being retold.

## *Discovering*

### Goals
To help the children understand what grain is.
To help the children learn what foods are produced from grain.

### BAGS OF SEEDS (3 AND 4-YEAR-OLDS)

### Description of Activity
The children compare and contrast different kinds of seeds, then use the seeds to create pictures.

### Materials
plastic bags, each of which contains a large number of one of the following: sunflower seeds, orange seeds, watermelon seeds, apple seeds, grape seeds, pumpkin seeds, avocado seeds (if possible)

construction paper
white glue

**Procedure**
1. After retelling the story, gather a small group of children together during free choice activity time.
2. Give a bag to each of the children and provide them with opportunities to discuss the contents of their bags, focusing on color, shape, size, the kind of tree on which it grows, etc.
3. Following this activity, encourage the children to share their seeds with each other as they create pictures. To make the pictures, they glue the seeds onto the construction paper in any way they wish.
4. Upon completion of procedures 1-3 above, repeat the activity with other small groups of children in the class, until all of the children have had an opportunity to participate.

## BAGS OF SEEDS (5 AND 6-YEAR-OLDS)

**Description of Activity**
The children observe changes in seeds over a month's time and record their observations.

**Materials**
a variety of seeds (lima beans, watermelon, sunflower, peach, plum, etc.)
plastic sandwich bags (3 or 4 per child)
several paper plates
paper towels
a large bowl of water
experience chart
felt marker

**Procedure**
1. Encourage the children to bring in a variety of seeds to the classroom.
2. During free choice activity time, gather a small group of children around a table containing the above materials. Place the seeds on paper plates to make them easily accessible.
3. Discuss what seeds need to help them grow. Explain that seeds need a moist environment in order to sprout.

4. Provide a plastic sandwich bag and a paper towel for each child.
5. Each child should wet his/her paper towel in the bowl of water and squeeze out the excess water.
6. The child then chooses a seed and places that seed and the paper towel into the sandwich bag.
7. If desired, children may choose to repeat this procedure with other kinds of seeds.
8. Instruct each child to close the bag securely and to label the bag with his/her name and the name of the seed on a piece of masking tape. Place the bags on a sunny window sill.
9. Repeat the procedure above with other small groups of children until all of the children have had an opportunity to participate.
10. The children should observe the seeds in their bags twice a week. Their observations should be recorded on an experience chart which also includes the date of the record.
11. After one month, observe the bags of seeds, note the changes, and compare these to the information previously recorded on the experience chart.

## *Experimenting*

### Goal
To help the children learn ways to store food and ways to keep food from spoiling.

### FOOD STORAGE (3 AND 4-YEAR-OLDS)

### Description of Activity
The children learn through observation some effective ways to store food.

### Materials
3 small flower pots
potting soil
water
experience chart
felt marker
grain ready for planting, such as barley, wheat berries, oat groats (purchase at a natural food store)

# Little Becomes Much

## Procedure
1. At circle time or in small groups during free choice activity time, discuss the story with the children, Stress the importance of not wasting food.
2. Show the children the three flower pots and do the following:
   a. Plant some grain in a container containing potting soil (with good drainage), and place it in a sunny window.
   b. Place some grain in a second container, cover the container, and place it in the refrigerator.
   c. Place some grain in a third container, and leave it uncovered on the science table.
3. After leaving the three containers for one week as described above, gather the children together and check the contents of each container. Discuss how the contents of each container look. Continue this activity for six weeks. Record the children's comments on an experience chart, as shown below:

> **Storing Grain**
> 1. When grain was planted in soil it _____ .
> 2. When grain was kept in the refrigerator it _____ .
> 3. When grain was left uncovered on the science table it _____ .
> 4.
> 5.
> 6.

## FOOD STORAGE (5 AND 6-YEAR-OLDS)

### Description of Activity
The children learn effective ways to store food. They observe and record information.

### Materials
3 small flower pots
potting soil
water
experience chart

felt marker
grain ready for planting, such as barley, wheat berries, oat groats (purchase at a natural food store)
large piece of poster board

**Procedure**
1. At circle time or in small groups during free choice activity time, discuss the story with the children. Stress the importance of not wasting food.
2. Show the children the three flower pots and do the following:
   a. Plant some grain in a container containing potting soil (with good drainage), and place it in a sunny window.
   b. Place some grain in a second container, cover the container, and place it in the refrigerator.
   c. Place some grain in a third container, and leave it uncovered on the science table.
3. After leaving the three containers for one week as described above, gather the children together and check the contents of each container. Discuss how the contents of each container looks. Continue this activity for six weeks. Record the children's comments on an experience chart, as shown on page 135.
4. Create a class graph. Post it, and enter the information weekly.

|        | Grain A | Grain B | Grain C |
|--------|---------|---------|---------|
| Week 1 |         |         |         |
| Week 2 |         |         |         |
| Week 3 |         |         |         |
| Week 4 |         |         |         |

## Food Experiences

### Goals
To help the children learn sanitary food handling practices.
To encourage the children to taste a variety of cereals.

## MAKING SNACK (3 AND 4-YEAR OLDS)

### Description of Activity
The children make a snack combining a variety of dry cereals.

### Materials
a variety of dry cereals (such as Wheat Chex, Rice Chex, Shredded Wheat, Rice Krispies, Corn Flakes, etc.)
3-5 large mixing bowls
3-5 large mixing spoons
a plastic bowl and a plastic spoon for each child in the class

### Procedure
1. After the children have washed their hands for snack, gather them together at the snack table.
2. Empty each kind of cereal into one of the large mixing bowls which is provided with a large mixing spoon.
3. Provide each child with a plastic bowl and a plastic spoon.
4. Encourage the children to prepare their own snack mixture from the contents in the large mixing bowls. When they have helped themselves and mixed the contents of their own bowls, they are ready to join their classmates in reciting the blessing over grains.

*Baruch Atah Adonai Eloheynu Melech Ha-olam Shehakol Neh'yeh Bidvaro.*

Blessed are You, Eternal our God, Ruler of the universe, by Whose word all things come into being.

## COOKING CEREAL (5 AND 6-YEAR-OLDS)

### Description of Activity
The children prepare cooked cereal in class and eat it at snack time.

### Materials
box of Wheatena or Oatmeal (or both)
saucepan
mixing spoon
burner

water (the amount requested on the box)
measuring spoons
measuring cups

**Procedure**
1. After the children have carefully washed their hands, gather a small group of them together.
2. Read and discuss the recipe on the box.
3. Write the key points of the recipe on an experience chart.
4. Following the recipe on the experience chart, prepare the cereal with the children.
5. When the cereal has been prepared, cover the bowl to keep it warm.
6. Gather other small groups of children together and follow instructions 1-4 (above) with each group. When all of the children have had an opportunity to cook their cereal, gather all of the children and eat the cereal for a snack. Serve with milk, white or brown sugar, and cinnamon.

## TAKING THE STORY HOME

1. **Story Starters**
Send home a list of story starters for the children to complete during carpool, at the dinner table, while taking a walk, etc.:
   Rabbi Pinhas Ben Yair opened the door and saw . . .
   The two men looked very . . .
   They were holding . . .
   They asked the Rabbi to . . .
   Rabbi Ben Yair told them . . .
   Rabbi Ben Yair put the grain . . .
   After he planted the grain, he saw that . . .
   When the men returned, they discovered that . . .
   The men were very happy because . . .
   The men took the grain and decided to . . .

2. *Torah Talk*
Send home copies of "Pharaoh's Dream" and "A Leader in Egypt" in *Torah Talk* by Yona Chubara, Miriam P. Feinberg and Rena Rotenberg, stories about Joseph's plans to conserve grain. Suggest that families read it together, tell it together, discuss it, draw pictures about it, act it out, and then read that story in the Bible. On another occasion, study another story in the same manner. make this a regular event for family get-togethers.

3. **Garden in a Pot**
   Families can create an indoor garden as follows:

   **Materials**
   a flower pot
   pieces of broken flower pots or large stones
   potting soil
   seeds (cherry tomatoes, marigolds, or miniature zinnias, etc.)

   **Procedure**
   1. Gather together all of the materials, and encourage the children in the family to participate actively in all parts of this activity.
   2. Place the pieces of broken flower pots or stones on the bottom of the flower pot. Explain that this is done so that the roots of the plants can "breathe" as they are watered.
   3. Place potting soil into the pot until it is 3/4 full.
   4. Read the instructions on the package to the child(ren). Then place several seeds into the soil.
   5. Then place a little more soil on top of the seeds and pat very gently.
   6. Water the new plants.
   7. Place the pot in a sunny spot.
   8. When the shoots begin to appear, thin out the plants.
   9. As you watch the seedlings grow, discuss the story read in class. Relate the story to the growing seedlings.

CHAPTER 13

# The Precious Jewel

## BEFORE TELLING THE STORY

It is sometimes difficult for young children to understand the importance of returning things which do not belong to them to the rightful owners. The desire to keep the object may well overcome a sense of doing the correct thing. Ask the children: How does it feel to lose something? Have you ever found something that was not yours? Did you return it to its owner? How did that person feel when you brought it back? What did he/she say to you?

## TELLING THE STORY

Many many years ago, Rabbi Shimon Ben Shetah lived in Jerusalem, in the land of Israel. He was a teacher. His students respected him, and they especially loved to sit and learn from him.

Rabbi Shimon was a poor man. It was hard for him to take care of his family with so little money. Almost every day after he finished teaching, Rabbi Shimon walked in the forest looking for gallnuts. As he found them, he popped them into a small bag which he wore around his waist. When his bag was full, he returned home to make ink from the gallnuts. Then he sold the ink at the market to get money to support his family.

One day, Rabbi Shimon thought to himself, "Walking back and forth to the forest takes a lot of time. I don't have enough time to study. I have to find a way to have more time for studying." He thought long and hard about the problem.

Finally he decided, "When I go to the market to sell my ink I will buy a donkey. Then, instead of walking to the forest, I can ride the donkey, and that will give me more time for studying."

And that was what he did. With the money he earned from selling his ink, he bought a donkey from a man in the marketplace.

Rabbi Shimon brought the donkey to his school and tied it to a post outside the front door. His students were very happy about the donkey. Now Rabbi Shimon would be able to ride to the forest and save time for studying.

When school was over, the students ran to see the donkey. They examined it carefully.

"What a nice tail this donkey has," said one student. "It looks like a strong animal," said another. "It can carry Rabbi Shimon back and forth to the forest," said a third. "Look! Look here!" shouted still another student. "There's a beautiful gem hanging around the donkey's neck! Rabbi Shimon can sell the gem and get so much money that he won't have to go to the forest to collect nuts anymore. Then he can study as much as he wants to."

The students were thrilled with their discovery. They ran into the school calling, "Rabbi Shimon! Rabbi Shimon! Come quickly! See what we found. A beautiful gem is hanging from the donkey's neck."

Rabbi Simon ran outside. He examined the gem. He looked very upset. "I can't keep this gem. I have to return it to the man who sold me the donkey. It doesn't belong to me." Then he got on the donkey and rode away, holding the gem, and shaking his head.

Rabbi Shimon rode back to the marketplace. There he found the man who sold him the donkey.

"Here, Sir," he said, "this precious gem must be yours. It was hanging around the neck of the donkey I bought from you."

"Oh, thank you, thank you, Rabbi Shimon," said the man. "You are a very good and honest man."

When Rabbi Shimon left the marketplace and rode back home on his donkey, he had a smile on his face. He knew he had done the right thing.

**Questions on the Story**
1. Why do you think Rabbi Shimon's students liked him?
2. Why was it hard for Rabbi Shimon to take care of his family?
3. Why did Rabbi Shimon walk in the forest?
4. Why did Rabbi Shimon buy a donkey?
5. What did the students find?
6. Why do you think Rabbi Shimon was upset when he saw the precious gem?
7. Do you think the students were right to tell Rabbi Shimon to keep the precious gem?

## THEMES IN THE STORY

### *Rabbi Shimon was an honest man*

Rabbi Shimon was very poor and his life would have been easier had he sold the precious gem. Nevertheless, he knew that it would not be right to do so because it did not belong to him.

*Bringing the Theme Closer*
- What does it mean to be honest?
- Have you ever done something that showed your honesty?

### *The importance of study*

Study is an important element in the observance of Judaism. Rabbi Shimon's life-style showed his adherence to this important Judaic value.

*Bringing the Theme Closer*
- What are things that we learn when we study?
- Who are some other scholars we talked about, (e.g., Hillel, Shammai, etc.)?

### *Rabbi Shimon's students cared about him*

The students wanted Rabbi Shimon to have enough time and money to enable him to study in a leisurely manner.

*Bringing the Theme Closer*
- How did the students show that they cared about Rabbi Shimon?
- How do you show that you care about your mother, father, sister, brother, grandparents, friends, etc.?
- What are some new things you can do to show that you care about these people?

## CREATIVE FOLLOW-UP

### *Retelling the Story*

#### Goals

To help the children understand what occupations are and why people have chosen different ones.

To increase the children's understanding of various occupational options and the role that such workers play in serving the community.

To help the children understand the importance of Jewish community helpers.

## WHAT'S MY PARENTS' LINE? (3 AND 4-YEAR-OLDS)

### Description of Activity
Through discussions and the use of photographs, each child and parent (or parents) share information with the class on the parent's occupation.

### Materials
Pictures of people at their jobs (parents can help by contributing to this collection)

### Procedure
1. Following the telling of the story, discuss Rabbi Shimon's occupation.
2. Encourage the children to describe their parents' occupations and ways in which these are similar to and/or different from Rabbi Shimon's.
3. Invite parents to come to the class to describe their occupations. Have them bring (or send in if they can't come to class) photographs with captions showing them at their work. Magazine pictures may also be used.
4. If parents work as professionals or volunteers for the Jewish community, encourage them to describe this involvement and to compare this work with Rabbi Shimon's work as a teacher of Judaism.
5. Come back to this activity periodically until all of the parents have had an opportunity to describe their work in some way.

## JEWISH COMMUNITY HELPERS (5 AND 6-YEAR-OLDS)

### Description of Activity
The children interview Jewish community helpers in their school building and report to the class on information acquired.

### Materials
tape recorder
experience chart
felt marker

### Procedure
1. Describe some Jewish community helpers to the children (Rabbi, Cantor, Executive Director of a synagogue, Jewish Community Center worker, social worker, kosher butcher, kosher baker, etc.).

2. Arrange for small groups of children to meet with Jewish community helpers in the school building to interview them.
3. Prior to meeting with the helpers, decide with the children on specific questions to pose, such as:
   a. What kind of school did you attend to prepare for your job?
   b. What do you like best about your work?
   c. Do you have to wear special clothes to work?
   d. How do you help people when you are at work?
4. The interviewers report back to the class on their findings which are written on an experience chart.
5. Go over the experience chart with the children.
6. Display the chart on the wall and review it periodically.

|  | Kosher Butcher | Kosher Baker | Rabbi | Cantor | Exec. Dir. of Syn. | Teacher |
|---|---|---|---|---|---|---|
| School attended |  |  |  |  |  |  |
| Like the best about work |  |  |  |  |  |  |
| Wears special clothes |  |  |  |  |  |  |
| How helps people |  |  |  |  |  |  |

## *Discovering Nature*

### Goals
To help the children understand the diversity of nature.
To encourage the children to think of new ways to use items found outdoors.
To help the children understand that everything found in nature has a purpose and a place.

## MAKING BERRY INK (3 TO 6-YEAR-OLDS)

**Description of Activity**
Children make berry ink which they then use to make prints.

**Materials**
blueberries or blackberries
a strainer
a wooden spoon
a bowl or wide-mouthed jar
aprons
toothpicks
yarn
straws
writing paper

**Procedure**
1. Ask all participants to put on an apron. Then pour some of the berries into the strainer which has been placed over the bowl or jar.
2. Children press the berries through the strainer with the spoon.
3. To make prints, older children can dip a toothpick into the berry juice use the toothpick to draw on the writing paper. Younger children can create designs by dipping a straw or piece of yarn into the juice and using the yarn to draw on the paper.

## LET'S TAKE A WALK (3 TO 6-YEAR-OLDS)

**Description of Activity**
Children go on a nature walk to collect materials and to think of new ways of using them.

**Materials**
paper bags

**Procedure**
1. Find an outdoor area where there are various items the children can collect.
2. During circle time, discuss how Rabbi Shimon looked for gallnuts in the forest and how he used the nuts for making ink. Explain that you will be taking a walk outdoors to search for items that can be used in new ways.

Suggest that they pick up things that are safe to touch, and that are pretty, interesting, and colorful while not destroying nature. Discuss the importance of not picking up waste that could be a health hazard. Discuss the concept of *bal tashchit* — not wasting or destroying.
3. Give each child a paper bag in which to place found items such as twigs, leaves, stones, and shells. Take the group outdoors.
4. When the children return to the classroom, form a circle. Have them show and describe the contents of their bags.
5. Relate the finding of objects to the gathering of gallnuts by Rabbi Shimon.
6. Discuss possible uses for the materials with the children (create a collage, make jewelry, decorate the classroom, set up an exhibit, etc.).
7. Help the children to use their materials in the ways they suggested.

## *Art Activity*

### Goals
To help the children appreciate the creative process involved in combining materials.
To provide information to the children about their birthstones.
To encourage the children to learn to appreciate the beauty of precious stones.

### MAKING JEWELRY (3 AND 4-YEAR-OLDS)

**Description of Activity**
The children make gem-like jewelry.

**Materials**
macaroni of various shapes
a variety of colors of paint
paint brushes
yarn
masking tape
scissors

**Procedure**
1. Gather a small group of children together during free choice activity time.
2. Discuss the gem found on Rabbi Shimon's donkey. Help the children to think of ways in which they can make gem-like items from materials in the classroom.

3. Provide all of the needed materials within easy reach.
4. Help the children to decide which jewelry items they wish to make.
5. Encourage them to paint the macaroni pieces.
6. When the macaroni pieces have dried, children may string them onto a piece of yarn. (To facilitate this, make a point at the end of the yarn by wrapping it with a piece of masking tape.)

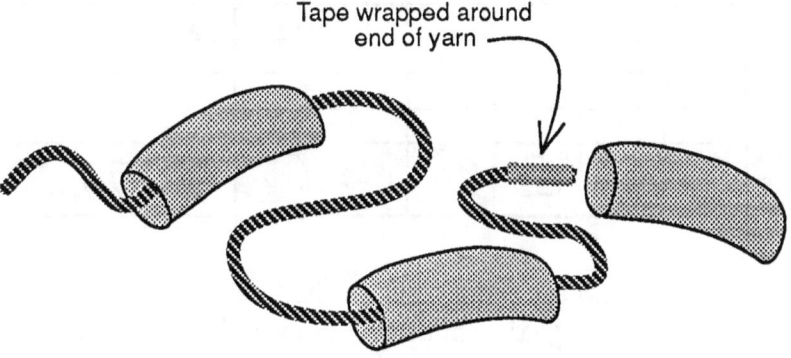

7. When all of the children have completed this activity, form a large circle. Children may show and briefly describe their creations to their classmates.

## BIRTHSTONES (5 AND 6-YEAR-OLDS)

### Description of Activity
Explain the association of a different birthstone with each of the months. Encourage the children to group themselves according to the sequence of months in the year. Then create a graph with information on the children's birth dates.

### Materials
pictures of birthstones for every month of the year
felt markers (in a variety of colors)
easel paper
construction paper

### Procedure
1. Explain the association of a specific birthstone with each of the months.
2. Display pictures of the birthstones and ask the children to group themselves according to the sequence of months in the year.

3. Solicit information from the children and write it on a chart as follows:

| | JAN | FEB | MAR | APR | MAY | JUN | JUL | AUG | SEP | OCT | NOV | DEC |
|---|---|---|---|---|---|---|---|---|---|---|---|---|
| | Josh | David | Sara | Max | Mollie | Steven | | Ron | Jon | | Avi | |
| | | Seth | | | Adam | | | | | | Judy | |
| | | | | | Debbie | | | | | | | |
| | | | | | | | | | | | | |
| | | | | | | | | | | | | |
| | | | | | | | | | | | | |
| | | | | | | | | | | | | |
| Pictures of Birth Stones | | | | | | | | | | | | |

4. Review the chart with the children.
5. Encourage the children to draw a picture of their own birthstone using felt markers and construction paper.

## TAKING THE STORY HOME

1. **Discussions**
   Encourage parents to talk with their children about their occupations and related subjects such as special training, special clothing, indoor or outdoor work, etc.

2. **Story Starters**
   Send home a list of story starters for the children to complete during carpool, at the dinner table, while taking a walk, etc.:
   Rabbi Simon's students loved to . . .
   Everyday, Rabbi Simon walked into the forest and . . .
   Rabbi Simon's students were happy for him because . . .
   When the students saw the jewel they . . .
   When Rabbi Simon saw the jewel he . . .
   After giving back the jewel Rabbi Simon felt . . .

3. **Making Jewelry**
   Suggest that family members make jewelry. Here are some ideas:

## a. Yarn bracelets

**Materials**
tape
cardboard strips
yarn (various colors)
paste

**Procedure**
1. Cut cardboard into strips that are about 1/2" x 7". Overlap the ends and tape them together to form a bracelet.
2. Tape one end of the yarn onto the cardboard. Then wrap the cardboard with the yarn, over and over, until no cardboard shows through. If more yarn is needed, tie on a new piece, knotting the ends on the inside of the bracelet and tucking in the ends.

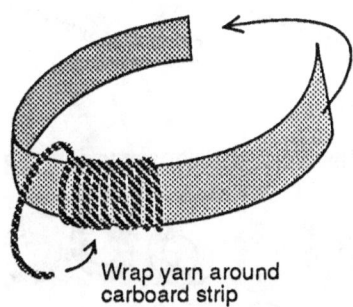

3. Finish the bracelet by dabbing paste onto the end of the yarn and tucking it underneath the wrapped yarn on the inside of the bracelet.

## b. Straws and cereal jewelry

**Materials**
straws
cheerios
fruit loops
construction paper
string or yarn
transparent tape
scissors

## Procedure
1. Cut pieces of string or yarn approximately 16" in length.
2. Wrap a piece of tape around one end of the string.

3. Cut the straws into small pieces.

4. Tie a small piece of straw or cereal onto the other end of the string.

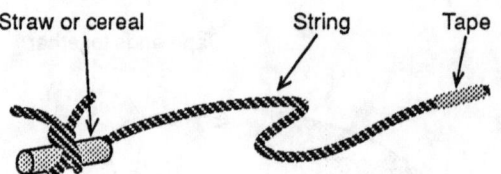

5. Cut small circles from the construction paper and make a hole in the middle.

6. Now you are ready to make a necklace or bracelet bringing together the pieces of straw, cereal, and construction paper circles.

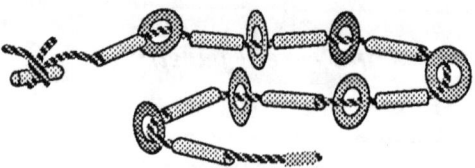

7. Tie the ends together when you have enough strung suit your needs.

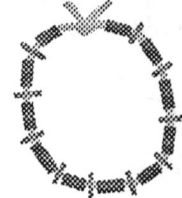

CHAPTER 14

# An Old Young Student

## BEFORE TELLING THE STORY

Discuss the fact that new immigrants need to study so as to learn the language and culture of their new country. Mention immigrants to the United States and to Israel and the great efforts they have undertaken to adapt to their new homes. Read *Mischa and Rachel* by Steve and Ilene Bayer and *Falasha No More* by Arlene Kessler.

## TELLING THE STORY

Eliezer ben Hyrcanus was twenty-two years old. He wanted to go to school. He wished so much that he could study Torah and learn about the Jewish people.

Eliezer's father was a very rich man, but he believed in working hard to get ahead. "You must go and work in the fields," he told his son. "There is no time for studying, and besides, you're too old to go to school now."

One day, as Eliezer was plowing the field, he made a decision. "I don't like this kind of work." He huffed and puffed as he pushed his plow along. "I want to study Torah. I'm so angry I could just cry!" And with that he sat on a rock, held his head in his hands, and moaned.

At that very moment, his father happened to walk by. "My goodness, Eliezer," said his father. "What happened? You're crying!"

"Father, I want to go to school," sighed Eliezer. "I need to study Torah and to learn about the Jewish people."

"But you're a grown man. You're too old to go to school," answered his father.

"I've made up my mind, Father," said Eliezer. "I'm going to school."

Then his father said, "It's more important for you to finish your work, so just get back to what you were doing," and he walked across the field shaking his head.

The next morning Eliezer woke up early, feeling sad but determined to get his work done. He went out to the field where he plowed and plowed all day long. Late in the afternoon as he was preparing to finish for the day, he suddenly tripped over a rock, fell down, and broke his leg.

# An Old Young Student

"Now I really won't be able to work in the fields," he said. "Maybe now I'll be able to go to school." His father heard him, but didn't answer.

A few days later, Eliezer was able to walk on crutches. He could only walk slowly. He packed a few things and left his father's house. He walked along the road very, very slowly. He kept going on his way, walking with the help of his crutches. He hadn't walked all that far, but he had been walking for a very long time, when he came to the town of Yavneh. He knew that there was a wonderful teacher in that town named Rabbi Yochanan ben Zakkai. He walked slowly, slowly, slowly on his crutches until he reached Rabbi Yochanan's school.

When he got there, Eliezar was disappointed to find that Rabbi Yochanan was nowhere to be found. "Oh, no!" he moaned. "How will I begin to study without a teacher?" and he sat down on the front steps to wait.

"I'll stay here and wait no matter how long it takes; even if it takes a day, even if it takes a week, even if it takes a month!"

And he waited, and waited, and waited, and waited, and waited. After he had waited for a very, very, very long time, Rabbi Yochanan finally returned.

"Rabbi Yochanan, Rabbi Yochanan," Eliezer called. "My name is Eliezer ben Hyrcanus. I am 22 years old. I have never gone to school. I've come from far away so that I might study with you. Please teach me the blessings, and also teach me how to read Hebrew so that I can study the Torah."

"Well, well," said Rabbi Yochanan. "You seem like a very serious student. I have a feeling that you will work very hard. Come to my school tomorrow so that we can begin studying. But first, I will teach you the *Sh'ma*. Repeat after me, *Sh'ma Yisrael Adonai Eloheynu Adonai Echad*."

Eliezer was so happy to be learning at last that he quickly and carefully said every word that Rabbi Yochanan taught him.

"Thank you, Rabbi Yohanan," Eliezer said beaming. "I'll be back tomorrow so that we can begin our work." And away he went, smiling from ear to ear.

From that time on, Eliezer slept at a small inn every night and studied with Rabbi Yochanan during the day. He couldn't have been happier, but he could have been less hungry.

One morning when he arrived at school, Rabbi Yochanan noticed how pale Eliezer was. "Have you eaten your breakfast yet?" he asked kindly.

"Oh, they serve breakfast every day at the inn where I'm staying," Eliezer answered. But he had not eaten breakfast in days. He didn't have enough money to pay for breakfast, so he came to school hungry day after day.

Rabbi Yochanan knew that something was not right. "Eliezer, from now on I think you should come and eat breakfast with me each morning so that we can begin our studies earlier," he suggested.

And from that time on, for the next three years, Eliezer ate breakfast with his teacher every day. As they ate they studied, and as they studied they ate.

Eliezer was a very good student. He studied Torah. He learned about Abraham, Isaac, and Jacob. He studied about Shabbat, Sukkot, and Pesach. He was excited to learn things that he had never learned before.

During all those years that Eliezer lived and studied in Yavneh, he never wrote a letter to his father. He felt sad that Hyrcanus didn't want him to study. All that time Hyrcanus knew that Eliezer was in Yavneh, but since he had not heard from him, he had no idea that Eliezer was such a wonderful student.

Hyrcanus was very angry with his son. Eliezer hadn't written to anyone back home. No one in his family knew anything about his life in Yavneh.

One day Hyrcanus announced to his family, "I must go to Yavneh for a little while," and off he went on his journey.

Rabbi Yochanan heard that Hyrcanus was coming to Yavneh. He had an idea. He planned a feast for his students and some invited guests. He sent an invitation to Hyrcanus, too.

On the day of the feast, many guests arrived, and so did Hyrcanus.

They all sat around a large table. Hyrcanus sat down, too. Then many students arrived and joined the guests at the table. There were so many people at the feast.

Before they ate, each of them said the blessing over bread — *Baruch Atah Adonai Eloheynu Melech Ha-olam Hamotzi Lechem Min Ha'aretz.* Then they ate the delicious food and enjoyed talking to each other.

After the meal, Rabbi Yochanan stood up. Everyone was quiet.

"I want to invite Eliezer to explain a certain part of the Torah," Rabbi Yochanan told the group. "He will tell you about Joseph and his brothers."

Eliezer was surprised to be invited to speak before such a large group of people. "No, Rabbi, please," he said. "I'm too shy to speak to all of these people."

But Rabbi Yochanan wouldn't listen to his protests. And the more Eliezer said he didn't want to speak, the more Rabbi Yochanan said, "You can do it. I know you can."

Finally, Eliezer stood up and began to speak. As he spoke, everyone in the room listened. The more he spoke, the more interesting he became, and the more people wanted to learn from him.

When Eliezer finished speaking, Rabbi Yochanan hugged Eliezer. "I'm so proud that you are my student," he said. "I knew you could do it, and you spoke even better than I thought you . . ."

But before Rabbi Yochanan could finish his sentence, Hyrcanus jumped up and ran over to Eliezer and hugged him.

"I am the luckiest and proudest of all fathers," he shouted. "I came here to Yavneh not knowing what would happen. I found my son, and he is a wonderful scholar and Rabbi. Who could be prouder than I am? Eliezer, I am sorry that I did not listen to you with my heart. I apologize that I have not helped you all these years."

Eliezer could not believe his eyes or his ears. He and his father hugged for a long time. They had missed each other very much! But they both realized that their separation had been for the best.

Now Eliezer, who had been a poor student for so long, was a famous Rabbi. And the money that his father gave him, he shared with his fellow students and with the poor people of Yavneh.

Eliezer felt rich to have made his father so happy. His father felt rich to have found his son once again.

**Questions on the Story**
1. Why did Eliezer's father think Eliezer was too old to go to school for the first time?
2. Where might a person go to school at the age of 22?
3. What kind of work did Eliezer do before he went to school?
4. Why did the Rabbi think it was important for Eliezer to eat breakfast?
5. Why was Eliezer's father surprised when he came to Rabbi Yochanan's for the feast?
6. Why were Eliezer and his father happy at the end of the story?

## THEMES IN THE STORY

### *The value of lifelong study*
Lifelong study is a Jewish pursuit, and, in fact, the *Sh'ma*, recited by Jews all over the world, commands us to study.

*Bringing the Theme Closer*
- Does your mom or dad go to school? What do they study?
- Are there classes for grown-ups in the building where you go to school? Do some of those classes meet on Saturday or Sunday when your school is not in session?

### *It's never too late to begin to study*
In Judaism, study can begin at any time. Adult Hebrew and Judaic studies classes are offered by synagogues and community centers.

*Bringing the Theme Closer*
- Has any grown-up in your family ever studied something?
- Have you ever taught a song or a poem to your mother or father?

### *The importance of helping a person achieve her/his goals*
In this story, Rabbi Yochanan helped Eliezer ben Hyrcanus achieve his goal.

*Bringing the Theme Closer*
- Has anyone ever helped you learn something, such as riding a tricycle or building with blocks?
- Have you ever helped someone else learn something?

# CREATIVE FOLLOW-UP

## *Retelling the Story*

### Goals
To help the children understand the sequence of events in the story.
To help the children understand the many feelings that are described in the story.

### FEELINGS (3 AND 4-YEAR-OLDS)

#### Description of Activity
The children express the feelings described in the story.

#### Materials
large paper plates
scissors
white glue
pictures of Eliezer — sad, nervous, happy, lonely; of Hyrcanus the father — angry, proud; of Rabbi Yohanan — happy (pictures showing emotions are provided on page 183)

#### Procedure
1. Photocopy the pictures on page 183. Then cut them out and spread them on a table accessible to the children.
2. Gather a few children together. Encourage each of them to select a picture and paste it onto a paper plate.
3. When all of the children have made a face, have them bring their paper plates and form a circle.
4. Begin to retell the story.
5. As you reach a part of the story that deals with a character's feelings, invite those holding a paper plate face to tell about their character, how he feels, and why.
6. Then continue telling the story until all of the children have had an opportunity to speak.

## FEELINGS (5 AND 6-YEAR-OLDS)

### Description of Activity
The children express the feelings described in the story by recording them as the teacher tells the story.

### Materials
tape recorder

### Procedure
1. Gather all of the children together in a circle.
2. Discuss and demonstrate appropriate responses to feelings with the children, e.g., happiness – laugh; sadness – cry; hunger – moan and groan; surprise – make short loud shouts.
3. Form groups of 2 to 4 children to express each of these emotions. Seat the children together and help them practice their responses to the emotions they choose to represent.
4. Turn the tape recorder on and begin telling the story. Pause when you reach a point where it is appropriate for a group of children to express an emotion. Point to the children in turn to elicit their responses.
5. After a few moments, continue telling the story, again stopping for appropriate responses.
6. After telling the whole story, listen to the tape recording.
7. Place the tape recorder and the recorded tape in the listening center and encourage the children to play it during free choice activity time.

## *Art Activity*

### Goals
To help the children empathize with others.
to provide a chance for children to do something for a person in need.

## WINDOW SHADE MURAL (3 AND 4-YEAR-OLDS)

### Description of Activity
The children create a window shade for Eliezer to keep in his new home to help cheer him up.

**Materials**
    a white window shade
    crayons
    felt markers

**Procedure**
1. During free choice activity time, gather 5 or 6 children together around a table with the materials above within easy reach.
2. Discuss the way Eliezer might have felt when he was working hard as a student and living in poverty. Ask the children to think of ways to help someone whose life is hard. Encourage each of them to speak while the others listen.
3. Unroll part of the window shade.
4. Encourage each of the children to decorate it with felt markers and/or crayons as they wish.
5. When this group of children has completed this task, invite another group to the table and repeat procedures 1-4.
6. Unroll the window shade an appropriate amount for each of the new groups.
7. Encourage those children who are able to do so to write their own names under their contribution to the project. Write the names of those who are unable to do so themselves.
8. Display the shade mural on the wall under a sign which says "A Gift For Eliezer's Home."

## JUNK SCULPTURE (5 AND 6-YEAR-OLDS)

**Description of Activity**
    The children create things that Eliezer might need when studying.

**Materials**
    collage materials (yarn, buttons, fabric pieces, colored paper, ribbons, tissue paper, etc.)
    empty toilet paper rolls
    empty paper towel rolls
    crayons
    felt markers
    egg cartons
    glue and/or tape

boxes of various shapes and sizes
construction paper
scissors

**Procedure**
1. Ask the children to bring empty boxes to school for this project. Send a note home for parents.
2. During free choice activity time, gather 5 or 6 children together around a table with the materials above within easy reach. Be sure that there is sufficient space in front of each child for working comfortably.
3. Discuss things which Eliezer might have needed in his new life as a student. Encourage each of the children to speak while the others listen.
4. Help the children to begin to make a creation of their own imagination for Eliezer.
5. When this first group has completed the task, invite other groups to the table and repeat the activity.
6. After all of the children have completed their creations, invite them to show and tell about them at circle time. If necessary, carry this activity over for more than one circle time in order to give each child an adequate amount of time to show and describe her/his creation.

## *Creative Writing*

### Goals
To help the children understand why Eliezer decided to go to school.

### FAN MAIL (3 AND 4-YEAR-OLDS)

### Description of Activity
The children draw pictures which they pretend to sent to Eliezer.

### Materials
drawing paper
felt markers
crayons

## Procedure
1. After telling the story, gather 4 or 5 children together.
2. Encourage each child to draw a picture to pretend to send to Eliezer.
3. Invite the children to dictate a message to accompany the picture and write it on the paper.
4. Display all of the pictures on a bulletin board under a label stating "Messages for Eliezer."

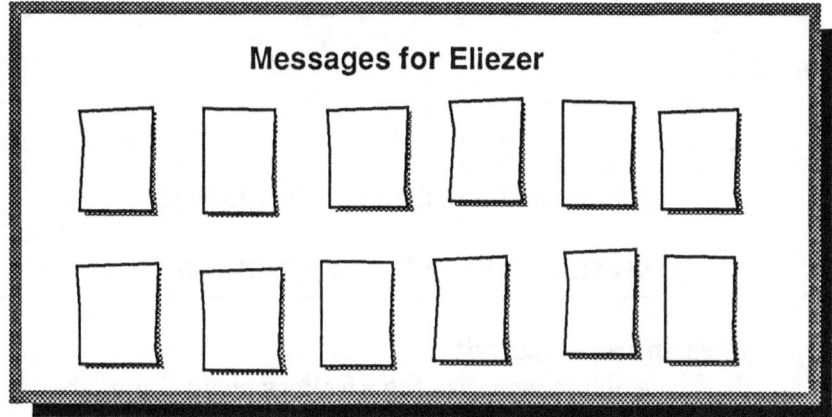

## LETTERS TO HYRCANUS (5 AND 6-YEAR-OLDS)

### Description of Activity
The children pretend to be Eliezer, writing letters to Hyrcanus from Jerusalem.

### Materials
felt markers
newsprint paper

### Procedure
1. During free choice activity time, gather a small group of children together.
2. Discuss letters which Eliezer might have sent to his father and information which he might have included in those letters.
3. Provide felt markers and newsprint paper for each child and encourage children to pretend to write the letters. Have each child write his/her name on their letter. If the children are not yet able to write, they may record their messages on tape.

4. Upon completion of this activity, repeat it with another small group of children until all of the children have had an opportunity to write at least one letter.
5. Encourage the children to share their letters with the entire class at circle time. Continue sharing the letters for several consecutive days until all of the children who wish to share their letters have had an opportunity to do so.

## *Show and Tell*

### Goal
To help the children talk about their feelings.

### SHARING GOALS (3 AND 4-YEAR-OLDS)

### Description of Activity
The children verbalize their feelings about things they have learned and things they would like to know more about.

### Materials
3 experience charts
3 felt markers (of different colors)

### Procedure
1. Gather the children together. Discuss the things they already know (addresses, phone numbers, birthdays of people in their families, things we do on Shabbat and Pesach, etc.), and the things they would like to know more about. Also, talk about the positive aspects of school and learning.
2. Write their responses on the experience charts, categorizing them as as shown on the next page.

| Things we know | Things we want to know | Good things about school |
|---|---|---|
| 1. | 1. | 1. |
| 2. | 2. | 2. |
| 3. | 3. | 3. |
| 4. | 4. | 4. |
| 5. | 5. | 5. |

   3. Display the charts.

## SHARING GOALS (5 AND 6-YEAR-OLDS)

### Description of Activity
The children discuss things they have learned and things they would like to know more about, as well as what they want to be when they grow up.

### Materials
3 experience charts
3 felt markers (of different colors)

### Procedure
1. Gather the children together and discuss things they already know (address, phone number, birthdays, ways to clebrate Shabbat and Passover, etc.) and things which they would like to know more about. Also, talk about the positive aspects of school and learning.
2. Encourage each child to act out what they want to be when they grow up without using words. The other children try to guess the occupation.

# TAKING THE STORY HOME

### 1. Story Starters
Send home a list of story starters for the children to complete during carpool, at the dinner table, while taking a walk, etc.:

Eliezer wanted to study Torah because . . .
His father wanted him to stay at home so that . . .
Eliezer wanted to meet Rabbi Yochanan because . . .
Before Eliezer came to school each day, he . . .
Rabbi Yochanan worried that Eliezer . . .
Eliezer's father was so surprised that . . .
Eliezer and his father were . . .

2. **Play a Feelings Game**
Photocopy the picture on page 183. Glue it to a firmer surface (such as poster board) and attach the spinner to the center. Each family member in turn spins the spinner. When the spinner stops at a particular picture, the person whose turn it is talks about the feelings expressed in that picture and how it relates to the story. The person also talks about times when he/she felt that emotion.

3. **Intergenerational Study**
Family members can study together, regardless of the range of ages. Babies, young children, parents, and grandparents all have something to contribute and to gain from the experience. Copy and send home a story from *Torah Talk* by Yona Chubara, Miriam P. Feinberg, and Rena Rotenberg. Suggest that families read it together, tell it together, discuss it, draw pictures about it, act it out, and then read that story in the Bible. On another occasion, study another story in the same manner. Make this a regular event for family get-togethers.

CHAPTER 15

# *The Good Teacher*

## BEFORE TELLING THE STORY

Help the children learn about the importance of treating others with kindness and respecting their feelings. Read *I Have Feelings* by Terry Berger and *I Was So Mad* by Norma Simon. Intersperse the readings with questions such as: How do you think that person felt? What could be done to make that person feel better about himself/herself and the situation he/she is in? What would you do if you were his/her friend?

## TELLING THE STORY

Hillel was a teacher. Everyone knew that he was a very good one. He always spoke kindly to his students. Students liked to study with him because he was very patient.

He taught his students about the Torah, about Shabbat, and about *tzedakah*. He tried very hard to answer all of their questions.

Once a student asked, "Hillel, do you think it was difficult for Abraham and Sarah to leave their home and go to Canaan?"

"I'm sure it was," Hillel answered, "but Abraham had faith in God. He knew that God would take care of him and Sarah in Canaan."

Shammai was also a teacher. He did not have as many students as Hillel had. He was not as patient with his students.

Once, Shammai's student asked, "Shammai, do you think it was difficult for Abraham and Sarah to leave their home and go to Canaan?"

"That's a silly question," Shammai responded, and he did not answer it. When the student heard Shammai's answer, he was afraid to ask another question.

One day, a man who was not Jewish came to Shammai's house. "Rap! Rap!" He knocked on the door.

"Who is it and what do you want?" asked Shammai as he opened the door.

"I would like to become Jewish," answered the man. Please teach me all about being Jewish while standing on one foot."

Shammai couldn't believe his ears! "What do you mean?" he shouted. "Do you really think that you can learn all there is to know about being

Jewish in so short a time? Go away! I have no time for this foolishness!" And Shammai slammed the door.

A little while later, the same man came to Hillel's house. "Rap! Rap!" He knocked on the door.

Hillel opened the door. "Hello," he said, "how can I help you?"

"I would like to become Jewish," said the man. "Please teach me all about being Jewish while standing on one foot."

"I will tell you the most important thing about being Jewish," said Hillel kindly. "Never do things to other people that you don't want done to you. Now you need to study hard in order to learn more about being Jewish."

The man listened carefully as Hillel spoke. Then he said, "I like what you have told me. Now I know something about being Jewish. I know that I need to study and learn a lot more. And I plan to take the time to do it."

**Questions on the Story**
1. What are some of the things Hillel taught his students?
2. How did Shammai answer the man's questions?
3. What did Hillel tell the man?
4. Which way of answering seems better to you?

## THEMES IN THE STORY

### Showing respect for the questions of others
Hillel answered his students' questions respectfully. Shammai did not. That was why students preferred to study with Hillel.

*Bringing the Theme Closer*
- Has anyone ever asked you a question that you thought was silly? Did you laugh or did you help that person find an answer?
- Did anyone ever laugh at your questions? How did this make you feel?
- Do your teachers listen carefully to your questions?

### Be helpful when someone wants to learn more
Hillel knew that the man who came to his door wanted to learn more about being Jewish so he directed him toward that information.

*Bringing the Theme Closer*
- Did you ever want to learn more about something?
- Who did you ask for help?
- What did that person tell you?

# CREATIVE FOLLOW-UP

## *Retelling the Story*

### Goal
To encourage the children to sequence the story.

## WHERE DO I BELONG? (3 AND 4-YEAR-OLDS)

### Description of Activity
The children draw and sort pictures about various events and characters in the story.

### Materials
3 manila envelopes
a very large sheet of poster board
drawing paper
felt markers
crayons

### Procedure
1. Before beginning this activity with the children, create a "Good Teacher" poster by mounting the envelopes on the poster board. Mark each envelope as follows:

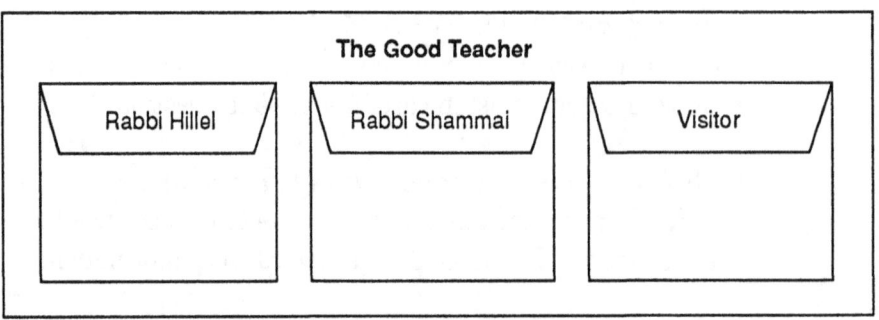

2. After telling the story, encourage the children to draw pictures about any aspect of the story or of the characters which they wish to illustrate. Suggest that the children place their illustrations in their cubbies until circle time later in the day.
3. Later, during circle time, place the "Good Teacher" poster near the seated children. Ask children to hold their story illustrations in their laps.
4. As each event or person in the story is mentioned, the children who are holding pictures of the event or person should place their pictures into the appropriate envelope.
5. After this activity is completed, place the poster board in a convenient area. Children may review the story on their own during free choice activity time.

## GARDEN GLOVE PUPPETS (5 AND 6-YEAR-OLDS)

### Description of Activity
The children make simple puppets to use during the retelling of the story.

### Materials
gardening glove (one for each child)
pieces of velcro
pieces of felt
white glue
scissors
felt markers

### Procedure
1. Gather a small group of children together during free choice activity time.
2. Provide all of the materials within easy reach.
3. The children cut 3 round pieces of felt to fit on each of three fingers (excluding the thumb) of the glove.
4. They then draw a face on each of the pieces of felt representing each of the three different characters in the story.
5. Provide each child with 6 pieces of velcro.
6. Each child glues one velcro piece on each of 3 fingers of the glove and on the back of each of the felt faces.

7. After they complete the gloves, encourage the children to tell the story to each other.
8. Each child can make a second garden glove puppet to take home or to keep in a story box.

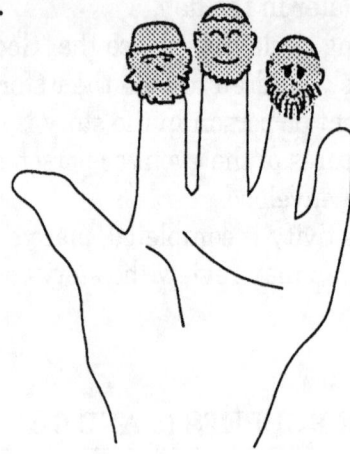

## *Game Time*

### Goal
To help the children review the Jewish information that they learned previously.

### BALANCE AND SAY (3 AND 4-YEAR-OLDS)

### Description of Activity
The children take turns responding to questions on Jewish topics while hopping on one foot.

### Materials
None

### Procedure
1. Gather all of the children together in a standing circle.
2. Ask one child to stand on one foot and respond to a question on a Jewish topic. Examples of questions:
   Where do we eat on Sukkot?
   What foods do you like to eat in the *sukkah*?
   What holiday comes every week?
   What kind of bread do you eat on Shabbat?

What do you light on Chanukah?
How many candles are on a *chanukiah*?
3. That child then chooses a successor.
4. Continue this activity for 10 minutes or until interest wanes.

## JUMP AND TELL (5 AND 6-YEAR-OLDS)

### Description of Activity
The children take turns leading the class in a physical activity while they talk about a Jewish subject.

### Materials
None

### Procedure
1. Gather the children together in a standing circle.
2. One child is chosen to enter the center of the circle and initiate a physical activity (hopping, bending, skipping, etc.).
3. While doing this he/she recites as much information on a selected Jewish topic as possible. For instance, you might ask:
What happened to Joseph when he went to Egypt?
What do you say before eating bread?
What blessing do you say before drinking wine or grape juice?
What do you do at a *Seder*?
4. The other children imitate the physical activity chosen by the child in the center of the circle.
5. After a while, encourage the child in the circle to stop and choose another child to be the leader.
6. Continue playing this game until all of the children have had a turn or until children are no longer interested.

# TAKING THE STORY HOME

### 1. A Conversation
Suggest to parents that at the Shabbat or holiday dinner table they include a Jewish topic in the conversation. For instance:
   a. Tell the children how the family acquired cherished Jewish ritual objects (*Kiddush* cup, candlesticks, *Seder* plate, etc.).

b. Read a story on a Jewish topic.
   c. Share some memorable Jewish experiences (your wedding, a family Bar/Bat Mitzvah celebration, interactions with a special Jewish relative or friend, etc.).

2. **Retell the Story**
   Using the garden glove which they decorated in class, the children can tell the story of the "The Good Teacher" which they learned in class.

3. **"What If?"**
   Parents can lead a family discussion on "what if?" questions related to the story, such as:
   What if someone asked you to tell him/her the most important thing about being Jewish?
   What if someone asked you to help them be Jewish?
   What if someone asked you to name the most fun Jewish holiday?
   What if someone asked you to help him/her make a Shabbat dinner? What would you say?

4. **Story Starters**
   Send home a list of story starters for the children to complete during carpool, at the dinner table, while taking a walk, etc.:
   Hillel was a teacher who . . .
   The thing that people knew about Shammai was that . . .
   When Shammai opened the door for the visitor, he . . .
   When Hillel opened the door for the visitor, he . . .
   The visitor asked about . . .
   The visitor was happy with Hillel's advice because . . .

CHAPTER 16
# Two Brothers

## BEFORE TELLING THE STORY

Discuss siblings and the ways that they relate to one another. How do they help each other? How do they hurt each other? Read stories of siblings and their relationships. Some suggestions:

1. *Torah Talk: An Early Childhood Teaching Guide* by Yona Chubara, Miriam P. Feinberg, and Rena Rotenberg
   After having been separated for 20 years, Jacob and Esau were able to forgive each other. (p. 85)
   Reuben showed concern for Joseph when his other brothers made plans to harm him. (p. 101)
   Miriam took care of her baby brother Moses and watched to see that no harm befell him. (p. 191)
   Aaron and Moses met in the desert after having been separated for many years, then acted together according to God's directions. (p. 219)
2. *What The Moon Brought* by Sadie Rose Weilerstein
   This book is a collection of holiday stories, all told within the context of a family which includes several children. The relationship between the children is clearly portrayed.
3. Some time between Purim and Passsover, introduce the concept of *Maot Chitim*. The purpose of such a fund is to provide the needy of the community with necessities for Passover. Many synagogues and other community organizations hold appeals for this fund. Send a note home to parents about this fund, explaining why it is needed, and encouraging them to become involved and to contribute.
4. *Different Kinds of Families* by Norma Simon. This book explores in words and pictures various kinds of families. Read the story and then discuss these families and compare them to the children's families.

## TELLING THE STORY

A long, long, long time ago, there were two brothers in Jerusalem. David lived with his wife Ruth and their children. Ezra was not married. He lived alone.

The brothers lived near each other; David in his house with his family on one side of a mountain, and Ezra in his house on the other side of the mountain.

Every morning, David and his three sons would say good-bye to the rest of the family and go out to work in their field. Together they would plow the fields, together they would remove stones to make the plowing easier, and together they would plant the seeds. Each day, when it was time for lunch, David and his three sons would sit under a shady tree and eat and talk and laugh together.

Every morning, Ezra would go out to work in his field. He would plow, he would remove stones, and he would plant. At lunch time, he would eat alone in the shade of an olive tree.

On Shabbat, Ezra would visit David and his family. Ezra, David, and David's family would eat, drink, sing, and talk together. They did this week after week, month after month, and year after year. They were all very happy with their lives. David liked being with his family. Ezra liked living alone. And the two brothers, David and Ezra, liked each other very, very much.

Every once in a while, David would say to his wife, "You know, Ruth, sometimes I worry about Ezra. He has no one to take care of him or to help him. I have you and our daughters and our sons to help me. The eight of us can get so much work done together! But Ezra is all alone. He has no one else. What would happen if we should have a bad year? What if the rains did not come, or if the wheat was destroyed by hail. Ezra would not be able to make it through the cold winter."

Meanwhile, on the other side of the mountain, Ezra would sometimes think about his brother. "David has to make sure he has enough food for Ruth and the children. What if there was a bad year in which the crops were destroyed? How would he and his family manage? I am only one person. I can always get along. But they are eight people, and that is a lot of mouths to feed."

One night, David could not sleep because he worried about Ezra. He worried and worried. Finally, he got out of bed, dressed, and went to his barn. He took several large bundles of grain from his grain pile and loaded them onto his wagon. He hitched his horse to the wagon and drove to Ezra's house. The moon was very bright as he reached his brother's barn. He quickly unloaded his grain and piled it on top of the grain in Ezra's barn.

Later that night, Ezra could not sleep. He was so worried about his brother! So, he got out of bed and went into his barn. He took several large bundles of grain from his grain pile and loaded them onto his wagon. He hitched his horse to the wagon and drove to David's house. When he reached his brother's barn, he quickly unloaded the grain and piled it on top of the grain in David's barn. He returned to his own home and before long was back in bed and fast asleep.

The next morning when each of the brothers went out to his barn he noticed something strange.

"My goodness!" exclaimed David, scratching his head. "How did my pile of grain get so big?"

"Look at that!" shouted Ezra, staring at his pile of grain. "My pile of grain has grown!"

Neither brother could understand how it was possible to take away grain at night, and still have the same amount of grain the next morning.

For the next few nights each of the brothers continued to wake up, go out to his barn, gather up some grain, take it to his brother's grain pile. Then, sure enough, each morning, when they went out to see their own grain pile, it was still the same size.

"My goodness!" each brother muttered to himself.

The brothers were very tired from their busy week of working during the day and getting up at night to take grain to each other's barn. They were so happy when Shabbat finally arrived and they were able to rest.

When Ezra arrived at David's house for Shabbat dinner, he was so tired that he could hardly keep his eyes open. When the family sat down at the dinner table, David felt as though he would fall asleep.

"What's the matter with you two?" asked Ruth. "You both look worn out!"

"I don't know," answered Ezra, shrugging his shoulders.

"I don't know either," said David, shaking his sleepy head.

"Well, I do," said David's oldest son, "I know exactly why. You see, one night, early this week, I was awakened by noises coming from our barn. I went to the window in time to see Abba driving away on the wagon loaded with grain. A while later he returned, but the wagon was empty. About an hour later, I was awakened again by noises near the barn. I went to the window just in time to see uncle Ezra in his wagon loaded with grain. He went into our barn and came out a few minutes later, but his wagon was empty. I didn't think much about it, at first. But then the same thing happened the next night and the next and the next. No wonder you two are so tired, you've been up in the middle of the night every night this week."

David and Ezra looked at each other's sleepy faces and started to laugh. "Aren't we silly!" laughed Ezra. "I was worried about you because you have such a big family to take care of. I didn't know whether you'd have enough grain to feed them all. So I wanted you to have some of mine."

"And I was worried that you wouldn't have enough grain because you don't have any helpers to work with you in your field. So I took some of our grain over to you."

And then the brothers laughed and hugged and laughed again. Everyone laughed with them. And everyone was very happy that they cared so much about each other.

When they all went to sleep that Shabbat night, they slept well, very well, indeed.

**Questions on the Story**
1. Did David need more or less than Ezra? Why?
2. What things did each of the brothers need?
3. Why was David so tired on Shabbat?
4. How did the brothers feel at the end of the story? What were the reasons for these feelings?

## THEMES IN THE STORY

*Family members show concern for each other in different ways.*
The brothers expressed concern for each other by sharing their grain, the product of their own hard work. David's family took care of Ezra on Shabbat because he had no family with whom to share Shabbat. David's wife and family were concerned that both brothers looked so tired. All members of the extended family in this story showed concern for each other in some way.

*Bringing the Theme Closer*
- What are some ways in which you can show concern for someone in your family?
- Have you ever been helped by a member of your family? How? How did you feel?

*There are different kinds of families*
David and his wife and children were one kind of family and Ezra was another kind. There are many different kinds of families.

*Bringing the Theme Closer*
- Describe your family. How many people are there in your family? How many are children? How many are adults?
- Do you know someone who has a different kind of family? What is that family like?

## CREATIVE FOLLOW UP

### Retelling the Story

#### Goals
To help the children sequence the events of the story.
To help the children internalize the story's concepts.

### BAG BROTHERS (3 AND 4-YEAR-OLDS)

#### Description of Activity
The children retell the story through the use of paper bags representing the brothers.

**Materials**
   brown paper lunch bags
   construction paper cut to the size of the lunch bags
   felt markers
   white glue

**Procedure**
1. After telling the story, gather a few children together at free choice activity time.
2. Encourage each child to make a picture on construction paper of each of the two brothers.
3. Then glue one of the pictures on each side of a lunch bag.

4. When children have completed the project, invite each of them to take turns talking about each of the brothers. With their hands in the bag, they hold up the bag to show one of the pictures. They tell something about that brother, then turn the bag and talk about the other brother.
5. Continue with this procedure until each of the children in the small group has had a turn to show and discuss "their" brothers. Then invite another small group of children to participate as the previous group has done.
6. Continue this activity until all of the children have had an opportunity to participate.

## PRINT PEOPLE (5 AND 6-YEAR-OLDS)

**Description of Activity**
   The children create pictures of the characters in this story, then use the pictures to retell the story.

**Materials**
an ink pad with red ink
light colored construction paper
black fine point felt markers
crayons

**Procedure**
1. After telling the story, gather a few children together at free choice activity time.
2. Give each child a piece of construction paper.
3. Show the children how to use the ink pad and make thumb prints on the paper.

4. Encourage the children to draw faces on each print with a felt marker.
5. Using crayons or felt markers, they can then add bodies to the faces.

6. Discuss the characters whom the children created and how each figures in the story.

7. When each of the children has had an opportunity to participate, invite another small group to participate.
8. After all of the children have participated, form a circle. Invite each child to show his/her pictures and to say one thing about them that relates to the story.

## *Play a Game*

### Goals
To help the children understand different roles which family members assume.
To help the children develop classification skills.

### WHICH DOESN'T BELONG? (3 AND 4-YEAR-OLDS)

### Description of Activity
The children make and play a game about different kinds of families.

### Materials
pictures of two men, with the name of each brother at the top
magazine pictures of families with children
magazine pictures of houses and rooms (in homes and offices) without children
scissors
white glue
poster board
card stock construction paper

### Procedure
1. Glue the two pictures representing the brothers onto poster board.
2. Encourage the children to bring in the magazine pictures described above.
3. Add additional pictures to assure that there is an adequate quantity for the project.
4. Gather a small group of children together at a table where all of the materials are within easy reach.
5. Help children paste each of the magazine pictures onto construction paper.

6. Now play the game as follows:
   a. Place the pictures of the brothers next to each other.
   b. Place in a pile in the middle of the table the pictures that are mounted on construction paper.
   c. Each child, in turn, takes a picture and decides whether to place it with the brother who has children or the one who lives alone.
   d. When all of the cards have been placed appropriately, encourage the children to place the cards in a pile in the middle of the table to give another group of children an opportunity to play. Children may play the game again during free choice activity time.

## WHOSE HOUSE IS IT? (5 AND 6-YEAR-OLDS)

### Description of Activity
The children create textured representations of the houses of the brothers in the story.

### Materials
a variety of colors of powered tempera paint
paste
one cup hot water
several tongue depressors or plastic spoons
approximately 40 pieces of construction paper, each cut into the shape of a house (some larger and some smaller) and shown as follows:

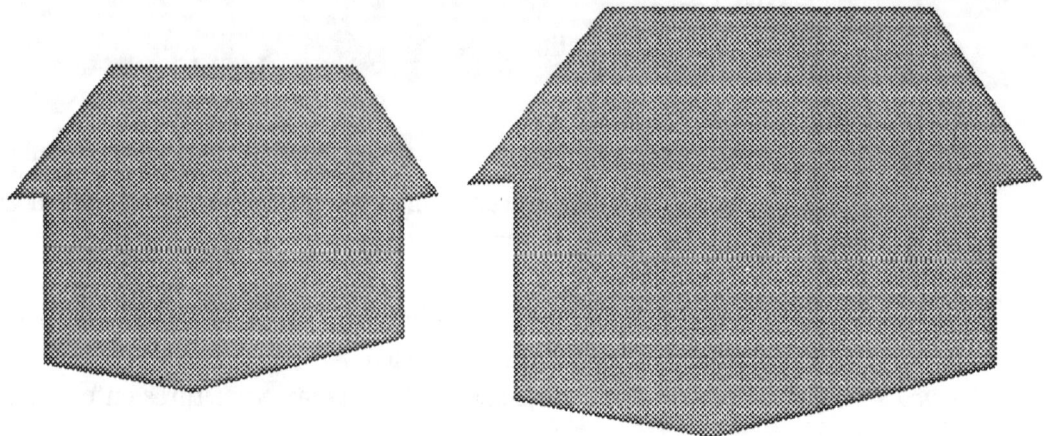

### Procedure

1. After retelling the story, gather together a small group of children during free choice activity time.
2. Place all of the materials within easy reach. Invite the chldren to help you create a thick paste-paint mixture as follows: Mix 3 tablespoons of paste with 2 tablespoons tempera paint. Add 2-3 tablespoons of hot water and stir until the mixture is smooth and thick.
2. Encourage each of the children to use the materials provided and to create and decorate as many representations of each of the brothers' houses as they wish.
3. Using a tongue depressor or spoon, the children apply the mixtures to the paper. The paper will have a textured look.
4. When the houses are finished, put them in a safe place to dry.
5. Invite other small groups of children to participate in this activity until all of the children have had an opportunity to do so.
6. After the houses have dried, the children should share them with each other at circle time, explaining to their classmates their rationale for creating them as they did.

## *Pantomime*

### Goals

To help the children develop a concern for other family members.

To help the children to understand the importance of helping others, as well as of asking others for help.

### I CAN HELP PEOPLE IN MY FAMILY (3 AND 4-YEAR-OLDS)

### Description of Activity

The children describe through pantomime some of the ways that they help their siblings.

### Materials

a tape recorder
an audiotape of Israeli music

**Procedure**
1. Gather the children together in a circle.
2. One child stands in the center of the circle.
3. Play the music.
4. While the music is playing, the child standing in the middle of the circle moves in pantomime showing ways that he/she helps a sibling.
5. Stop playing the tape and the child "freezes."
6. The other children try to guess what the child in the middle of the circle is doing, how the child is helping the sibling, etc.
7. The child who guesses correctly (or most closely) exchanges places with the previous pantomimer. The game then continues as previously.
8. Continue playing in this way until all of the children have had a turn, or until the children are ready to move on to another activity.

## I CAN HELP PEOPLE IN MY FAMILY (5 AND 6-YEAR-OLDS)

**Description of Activity**
Following a discussion about ways children can be helpful to their family members, parents send in notes describing ways their child has been helpful at home. The notes are read, discussed, and displayed.

**Materials**
felt marker
push pins
newsprint paper
poster paper

**Procedure**
1. During circle time, discuss with the children the importance of helping family.
2. Send home a letter requesting that parents send in notes as often as possible detailing ways that their child has helped family members. (Those children whose parents forget to send the notes can dictate into a tape recorder, describing ways that they helped family members.)
3. During circle time each day, read to the class the new notes from parents.

4. Make a chart with the names of each child. Then, as shown below, attach each of the notes to the chart next to the appropriate child's name.

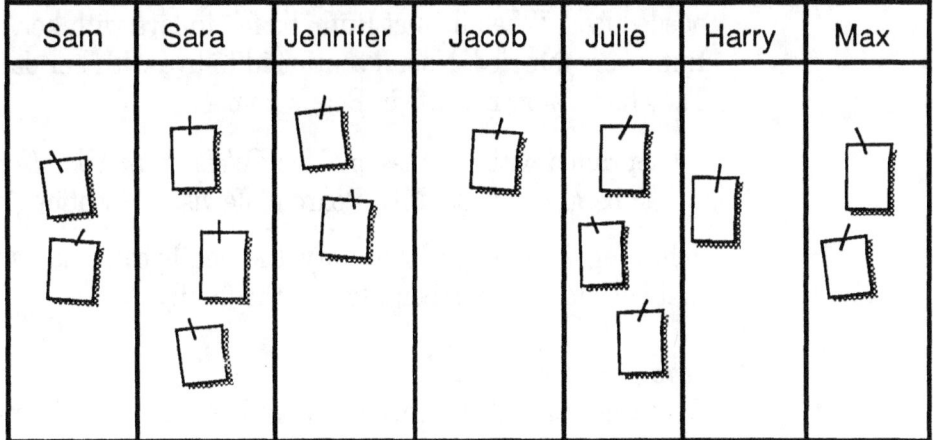

## TAKING THE STORY HOME

### 1. Telling the Story

Encourage parents to tell the story of Ruth and Naomi to their children and then to discuss ways their family members help each other. Before telling the story, they might read it in the Book of Ruth in the Bible. A good and fairly recent English translation will make the reading more fluent and fun.
If parents prefer, they can refer to the retold version that follows:

A long, long time ago, Naomi lived with her daughter-in-law Ruth in the land of Moav. Her husband had died, and Ruth's husband had died, too.

"I need to return to my home in Bethlehem, in the Land of Israel," Naomi told Ruth. "Now that I am old, I must leave you and go to be near my people. You should stay here in Moav."

"Oh, no," cried Ruth as she hugged Naomi. "I don't ever want to leave you! I will go with you. Your people will be my people." So Ruth and Naomi went together to the Land of Israel.

When the two women finally reached Bethlehem, they were tired and hungry. They had no money to buy food. "I have an idea," suggested Ruth. "Since this is the beginning of the barley harvest, I will go to the barley fields and pick up the grain that was left behind by the farmers. Since poor people are allowed to pick up the grain left on the ground, the farmers won't mind. Then we will have food."

"What a wonderful idea!" laughed Naomi.

Ruth worked hard in the fields and made sure that she and Naomi had enough to eat. The women took care of each other.

Boaz, the owner of the field, was happy to share his barley with those who needed food. When he met Ruth, he fell in love with her. After a while, he and Ruth were married. Naomi continued to live with her daughter-in-law Ruth. They had a very nice life in Boaz's home.

(Reprinted with permission from *Celebrate in Your Home* by Miriam P. Feinberg, Rockville, MD: Board of Jewish Education, 1990)

Following the telling of this story, the family can discuss the special things that each family member offers to the family.

2. ***Maot Chitim* Fund**
Encourage parents to learn about and become actively involved in a class or school *Maot Chittim* fund to raise money so that all Jews, whatever their resources, can observe Passover. Families might help to set up such a fund, raise money for it from others, and then help to distribute the food.

3. **Library Visits**
Suggest to parents that they accompany their children to the library to look for books on topics mentioned in the story, such as sibling relationships, sharing, and helping others in need. Some suggestions:
*Help: Getting To Know About Needing and Giving* by Laura Greene (the concept of needing and giving help)
*My Special Friend* by Floreva Cohen (the special relationship between a boy and his special friend, a child with Down Syndrome)
*My Brother's Bar Mitzvah* by Janet Gallant (the preparations for and celebration of a sibling's Bar Mitzvah)

# CHAPTER 17
# *Visiting a Sick Friend*

## BEFORE TELLING THE STORY

Discuss the importance of visiting the sick. Read and discuss the concepts in the following books by Jane Watson, Robert Switzer, and J. Cotter Hirschberg: *My Friend the Doctor* and *My Body and How it Works*.

Help the children understand the difference between people who are sick because they were injured and are therefore not contagious, and those who are sick because of an illness which others can catch. Brainstorm ways to help a contagious person get better, even though we can't visit him or her.

Contact a local hospital to request a speaker to speak with the children about hospitals and hospitalization. Following the speaker's presentation, ask the children: How does this person help to keep us healthy? What kind of medical instruments and/or medicine does the person use to do this? What kinds of things have we learned from this person about how to keep ourselves healthy?

## TELLING THE STORY

"Where is Miriam?" asked Mrs. Cohen, her teacher. "Children, have you noticed that she isn't here today?"

"That's right," agreed Aaron. "I noticed it right away when I came to school this morning."

"Me, too," nodded Shoshana. "She's always either the first or the second person in the class. I wonder where she is."

Just then, a student came in from the principal's office. "Miriam's mother just called the office to say that Miriam hurt her leg very badly this morning. She needs to stay home until the doctor gives her permission to come back to school."

"I'm sure that Miriam is very disappointed to be missing school," said Mrs. Cohen. "I know how much she loves being here. And if she hurt her leg badly, she's probably in pain, too. I wonder if there's something we might be able to do to cheer her up."

"How about making a get well card for her from all of the children in the class?" suggested Rachel.

"That's a really good idea, but how will we get it to her?" asked Mrs. Cohen.

"I can drop it off on my way home," offered David. "She lives just a few houses down the street from me."

So all the children got busy drawing and cutting and pasting and writing, until they had created a very special get well card for Miriam. They all signed it, and David delivered it on his way home.

After a week had passed and Miriam was still not back in the classroom, Mrs. Cohen reminded the children, "Miriam is still sick at home. Let's not forget that we need to help her feel better. What can we do for her now?"

The children thought and thought. Then Aaron had an idea. "Maybe someone can bring her a present from the class to help her feel better."

"I have some pretty flowers growing in my garden at home," suggested Joshua. "I know that my parents will be happy for me to share a few of them with Miriam. Maybe my mom will take me to Miriam's house after school today, so that I can bring them to her."

"Excellent idea!" smiled Mrs. Cohen. And everyone agreed it was the best idea of the day.

After another week had passed and Miriam had still not returned to school, Mrs. Cohen told her students, "Children, I'm concerned that Miriam hasn't been in school for two weeks. Her mother called to tell me that Miriam is lonely and uncomfortable. She suggested that anyone from our class who wants to visit her can do so after school tomorrow. I'm going to visit her. Maybe some of you can join me with your parents. When we visit a sick person, we help take some of the pain away."

The next day, when school was over, Mrs. Cohen and some of the children and their parents visited Miriam.

What big smiles all of the children and their parents and Mrs. Cohen had! But the person with the biggest smile of all was Miriam. Everyone had cookies and juice. Then the children told Miriam about all the things that had gone on in the class during the past two weeks. Then they sang some songs from school that everyone knew.

After a while, it was time for the guests to go home. As they were about to leave, Miriam announced, "I feel much, much better now, even well enough to go to school tomorrow. May I do that, Mom?"

"Of course, Miriam," laughed her mother. "You really will be ready to go back tomorrow, and all of your friends have made you feel ready. Thank you all for helping Miriam feel better."

"Good-bye, Miriam," her friends called to her as they left. "See you tomorrow!"

"See you tomorrow," called Miriam. "And thanks for helping me feel better!"

The next day, Miriam was back in school. She was so happy to be there with her friends again!

### Questions on the Story
1. Why couldn't Miriam come to school?
2. What was the first thing the children did to help Miriam feel better?
3. What other things did they do for Miriam?
4. How did Miriam feel after her classmates visited?

## THEMES IN THE STORY

### Showing concern for others
Mrs. Cohen and her students were concerned because Miriam had not been to school for several days. They discussed ways to show this concern and came up with a plan.

*Bringing the Theme Closer*
- Have you ever missed school because you were sick?
- Did someone show concern for you? In what way?
- Have you ever shown concern for someone else who was ill?

### Keeping oneself healthy
Miriam stayed home from school because she was injured. While she was there, she did many things to improve her health. Moses Maimonides (also known as the Rambam), a twelfth century statesman, physician, and Jewish philosopher, stressed the importance of keeping one's body in good health.

*Bringing the Theme Closer*
- What are some things that you do to stay healthy?
- How do people in your family help you do those things?
- What are some things that help you to get better when you have a cold?

### *There are many ways to help a sick or injured person get better*

Mrs. Cohen and her students knew that they could help Miriam get better by visiting her, bringing her pretty flowers, singing with her, and talking with her about school events. Rabbi Akiva taught us that by visiting a sick or injured person we help remove some of the pain that person feels.

*Bringing the Theme Closer*
- What can you do to help a friend who has a cold feel better? Someone with a broken bone?
- When should you not visit a sick person?
- Do you think you should ask an adult for help when planning an activity for a sick or injured friend? Why or why not?

# CREATIVE FOLLOW-UP

## *Retelling the Story*

### Goals
To help the children understand the sequence of events in the story.
To help the children internalize the story concepts.

### FILLING A SHOPPING BAG (3 AND 4-YEAR-OLDS)

### Description of Activity
The children retell the story using pertinent pictures from magazines.

### Materials
a large shopping bag (with handles)
magazine pictures relevant to the story (flowers, get well cards, someone sick in bed, etc.)
construction paper
scissors
white glue

### Procedure
1. After telling the story, ask the children to bring from home magazines which might contain pictures relevant to the story. The next day, add these to the ones you have collected.

2. Gather a small group of children together during free choice activity time. Place the materials within easy reach.
3. Help the children select appropriate pictures, cut them out, and glue them onto pieces of construction paper. After the glue has dried, place the pictures into the shopping bag.
4. Repeat this activity with other small groups of children until everyone has had an opportunity to contribute to the shopping bag.
5. Later, form a circle with all the children, and begin retelling the story.
6. As the story is being retold, pass the bag around the circle. Each child picks a picture from it and tells how the picture fits into the story.
7. Continue this activity until all of the children have had an opportunity to participate. If the children become restless, resume it at a later time.

## MAKING A BOOK (5 AND 6-YEAR-OLDS)

### Description of Activity
The children create a class book as a gift for a classmate who is ill.

### Materials
construction paper
drawing paper
crayons
felt markers
paper fastener

### Procedure
1. After telling the story, inform the children that they will create a book for a classmate who is ill. Suggest that each of them draw a picture about the story and/or dictate a joke or riddle to be written down in the book.
2. Later, during free choice activity time, gather together a small group of children. Help them to create a contribution (or several if they wish) to the class book.
3. If the children choose to tell a joke or riddle, encourage them to dictate as you write. Examples of riddles are as follows:
Why did the man throw the clock out the window?
Answer: To see time fly.
What has ears but can't see?
Answer: An ear of corn.

4. The children may illustrate their drawings, jokes, and riddles if they wish.
5. After each of the children has had an opportunity to contribute to the book, those who wish to do so can create a cover for the book. Include the recipient's name on the book cover (for example, "Rachel's Book").
6. Laminate the pages of the book and the cover. Then fasten them together with a paper fastener in the top left-hand corner.
7. Read the book to the class at circle time so that they may also enjoy this gift.

## *Learning Good Health Habits*

### Goal
To encourage the children to appreciate the importance of developing good health habits.

### HEALTHY HABITS (3 AND 4-YEAR-OLDS)

#### Description of Activity
The children discuss good health habits and ways to develop them.

#### Materials
magazines
poster board
construction paper
white glue
scissors
felt markers
paper fasteners

#### Procedure
1. Send home a note requesting that parents send in magazines containing pictures showing good health habits (for example, using tissues to blow one's nose, eating healthy foods, washing hands, etc.).
2. Gather a small group of children together during free choice activity time.
3. Discuss good health habits.
4. Provide all of the materials in an easily accessible location, and encourage the children to search for pictures that show good health habits.
5. Help the children to paste the pictures onto construction paper.

6. When the group has finished finding and pasting, help them to classify the pictures according to specific health habits. Make books with the pictures which have been placed together according to a theme (eating healthy foods, using tissues, etc.).
7. Help each child fasten their pictures together with paper fasteners.
8. Encourage the children to make covers for their books using construction paper and other materials.
9. Invite other groups of children in the class to participate in this activity until all have had an opportunity to participate.
10. Encourage the children to show and describe their book during circle time.

## COMMUNITY HELPERS WHO HELP US STAY HEALTHY (5 AND 6-YEAR-OLDS)

### Description of Activity
The children describe the work of various health professionals by using pictures relating to those people and their work.

### Materials
pictures of people in health professions (doctor, dentist, physical therapist, nurse, etc.)
white glue
several boxes with lids (shoe boxes or other boxes of similar size)
felt markers
construction paper

### Procedure
1. Label each of the boxes with the title of a health professional.
2. Gather 3 or 4 children together during free choice activity time.
3. Place all of the materials in an easily accessible area.
4. Discuss the various health professionals and the work which they do to help us stay healthy.
5. Encourage the children to paste pictures of the health professionals onto construction paper. Help them place their pictures in the correct box according to its label. Those who wish to do so may draw their own pictures of health professionals.
6. Gather together other small groups of children and repeat this activity until all of the children have had an opportunity to participate.

7. During circle time, place the boxes in the middle of the circle. Then invite each child to pick a paper from one of the boxes and describe it.

## *Creative Expression*

### Goal
To help the children to express non-verbally some ways that they can help a sick person.
To help the children understand the difference between an illness which is contagious and one which is not.

### HELPING A SICK FRIEND (3 AND 4-YEAR-OLDS)

### Description of Activity
Using a tape recorder, children discuss how their behavior might differ toward someone with a contagious disease and toward someone whose illness is not contagious. Then they show ways they would help both individuals.

### Materials
tape recorder
a tape with Israeli music (folk songs, dances, etc.)

### Procedure

1. Gather all of the children together in a circle.
2. Discuss the difference between contagious and non-contagious diseases, and when it is appropriate and desirable to visit people who are ill.
3. In turn, the children stand in the center of the circle and move to the music played on the tape recorder. As the music plays, the child pantomimes some ways to help a sick person.
4. Stop the music. The pairs "freeze," and the other children try to guess what the mime was portraying.
5. The child who guesses correctly (or makes the closest guess) chooses a partner. They then change places with the children in the circle. The game continues as previously described.

## HELPING A SICK FRIEND (5 AND 6-YEAR-OLDS)

**Description of Activity**
Children make a story tape for someone who is ill.

**Materials**
tape recorder
experience chart
felt markers

**Procedure**
1. Gather all of the children together in a circle.
2. Discuss the difference between contagious and non-contagious diseases, and when it is appropriate and desirable to visit people who are ill.
3. Suggest to the children that they may visit people who are ill with their voices, and that the class will make a story tape. Suggest that the children ask their families what is the best story to tell on the tape.
4. On a subsequent day, ask each child to record on the experience chart the story he/she wishes to tell on the tape.
5. Give each child a turn to tell a story into the tape recorder. The child should state his/her name and the title of his/her story.
6. When the tape is completed, and when everyone who wishes to do so has told a story, make several copies of the tape to used as desired.

## *Gifts for Sick Friends*

**Goals**
To help a sick person feel better.
To help the children understand how a person might feel who is isolated due to sickness.

## LET'S MAKE JEWELRY (3 AND 4-YEAR-OLDS)

**Description of Activity**
The children make gifts to give to a sick friend who needs cheering up.

### *Necklaces and Bracelets*

**Materials**
    macaroni
    rubbing alcohol
    strainer
    food coloring
    pint jar
    paper towels
    yarn
    transparent tape

**Procedure**
1. Combine 1/4 cup rubbing alcohol and as much food coloring as desired (experiment with amounts until you are satisfied) into the pint jar.
2. Add the macaroni to the jar and shake until the desired color is attained.
3. Empty the contents of the jar into a strainer.
4. Spread the macaroni out on paper towel and allow to dry.
5. Dye other pieces of macaroni with other colors of food coloring using the procedure described above.
6. When the macaroni is dry, and you have as many colors as you wish, wrap tape around the end of a piece of yarn.
7. String one macaroni with the yarn and tie the other end of the yarn around it.
8. String other macaroni pieces onto the yarn until the desired effect is achieved. Create a necklace or a bracelet.

### *Foil Rings*

**Materials**
    pieces of foil cut into 4" squares
    sequins
    buttons
    scissors
    felt markers
    white glue

### Procedure

1. Provide each child with a piece of foil.
2. Each child wraps the foil around a finger, joining the ends and twisting them to secure them closed.
3. Each child then decorates the ring using felt markers, then glues on the sequins and buttons.

## HANDY HANGERS (5 AND 6-YEAR-OLDS)

### Description of Activity

The children make a personalized gift to give to a sick friend.

### Materials

a wooden coat hanger (one per child)
metal cup hooks (5 per hanger)
white glue
scissors
an assortment of decorations (fabric pieces, yarn, ribbon, dried flowers, etc.)

### Procedure

1. Gather a group of 3 or 4 children together during free choice activity time.
2. Help each of the children to select a hanger and five cup hooks.
3. Help children to screw the cup hooks into the bottom of the hanger.
4. Encourage the children to decorate the hangers in any fashion they choose, using the materials which have been placed within easy reach. The gift is now ready to give to a friend who needs cheering up.

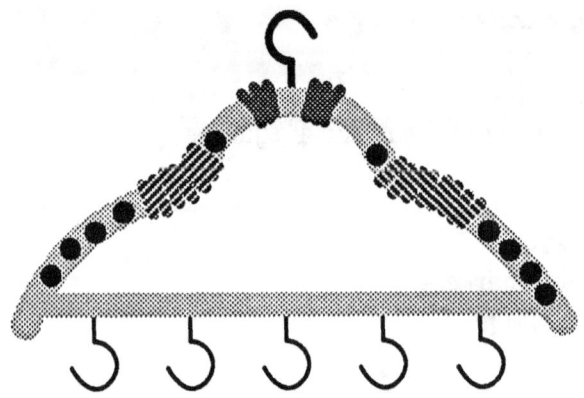

## TAKING THE STORY HOME

### 1. Sick in Bed
Family members can work together to create items that show a sick person how much they care about him/her.

*Muffin Tin Treasure Organizers*
After decorating the muffin tin with stickers, place colorful paper cupcake liners in each muffin container. The Treasure Organizer can be given to a family member or sick friend for storing items that might otherwise get lost during the illness.

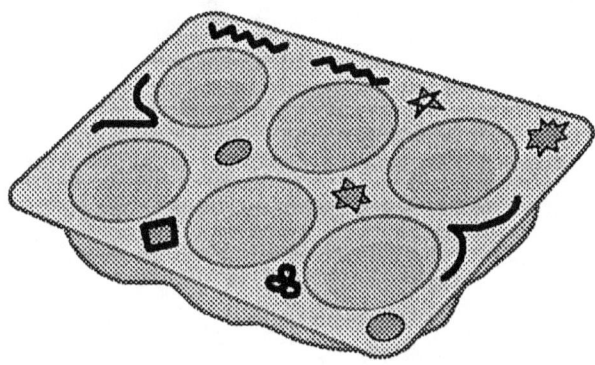

*Picture Puzzle Fun*
Cut out an interesting and colorful picture from a magazine. Glue it onto a piece of cardboard cut to the same size. After the glue has dried, cut the picture into 4 to 10 pieces, depending upon the age and skill level of the recipient. Using stickers and felt markers, decorate an envelope. Place the puzzle into the envelope and give it to a sick friend to help cheer her/him up.

# BIBLIOGRAPHY

## *For Adults*

Bialik, Hayyim N., and Yehoshua N. Ravnitzky. *The Book of Legends Sefer Ha-aggadah*. William G. Braude, trans. New York: Schocken Books, 1992.

> This is a translation of the Hebrew classic *Sefer HaAggadah*, a book of legends from the Talmud and the Mishnah, many of which are the sources of the stories in *Lively Legends*.

_____. *Stories of the Sages*. Chaim Pearl, trans. Tel Aviv: Dvir Publishing House, 1991.

> These are stories from the section of *Sefer Ha-aggadah* entitled "Stories of the Sages." All are from the post-biblical period.

Chubara, Yona; Miriam P. Feinberg; and Rena Rotenberg. *Torah Talk: An Early Childhood Teaching Guide*. Denver: A.R.E. Publishing, Inc., 1989.

> Three early childhood experts retell Bible stories from Abraham through Moses with accompanying activities that can be done at school and at home.

Feinberg, Miriam P. *Celebrate in Your Home*. Rockville, MD: Board of Jewish Education of Greater Washington, 1990.

> Written by an early childhood consultant, this book contains stories about the Jewish holidays for parents.

Frankel, Ellen. *The Classic Tales: 4,000 Years of Jewish Lore*. Northvale, NJ: Jason Aronson, 1989.

> This is a comprehensive collection of Jewish folktales beginning with biblical legends, and continuing through the Talmudic period.

Furfine, Sandy S., and Nancy Cohen Nowak. *The Jewish Preschool Teachers Handbook*. Denver: A.R.E. Publishing, Inc., 1991. (Revised Edition)

> This book contains chapters on teaching Jewish values, holidays, symbols, and Hebrew, as well as ideas for enriching the classroom environment and involving parents; contains an excellent bibliography.

Geras, Adele. *My Grandmother's Stories — A Collection of Jewish Folk Tales.* New York: Alfred Knopf, 1970.
> This is a collection of Jewish folktales by and about the author's grandmother.

Kargon, Marcia R. *Recipes and Jewish Cooking Experiences for Pre-School.* Baltimore: Board of Jewish Education, 1983.
> Chock full of holiday recipes, and featuring guidelines for cooking them with children, this book contains many recipes suitable for use with *Lively Legends.*

Kolatch, Alfred. *Complete Dictionary of English and Hebrew First Names.* Middle Village, NY: Jonathan David Publishers, 1984.
> An interesting book that includes the derivation and meanings of first names for both boys and girls, as well as the many forms of different names.

Miller, Karen. *The Outside Play and Learning Book.* Mt. Ranier, MD: Gryphon House, 1989.
> This book is filled with a variety of outdoor activities for young children.

Redleaf, Rhoda. *Open the Door, Let's Explore.* Minneapolis: Toys 'n Things Press, 1983.
> Suggested field trips within a neighborhood are described in this excellent book.

Rockwell, Robert E.; Elizabeth A. Sherwood; and Robert A. Williams. *Hug a Tree.* Mt. Ranier, MD.: Gryphon House, 1983.
> A variety of outdoor activities suitable for young children are described in this book.

Rotenberg, Rena, and Rachel Meisels. *Gmilut Hasadim Curriculum Guide — Early Childhood Level.* Baltimore: Board of Jewish Education, 1989.
> This book, written by an early childhood consultant and a teacher, covers in detail some aspects of *gemilut chasadim* (acts of loving-kindness).

Schram, Peninnah. *Jewish Stories One Generation Tells Another*. Northvale, NJ.: Jason Aronson, 1987.

>Herein is a wonderful selection of Jewish folktales retold by a masterful storyteller.

Schwartz, Howard, and Barbara Rush. *The Diamond Tree: Jewish Tales from Around the World*. New York: Harper Collins, 1991.

>This book includes a variety of legends and stories from Jewish communities around the world.

Schwartz, Howard. *Elijah's Violin and Other Jewish Fairy Tales*. New York: Harper & Row, 1983.

>Here are stories from a wide variety of sources (Egypt, Morocco, India, Persia, etc.).

_____. *Miriam's Tambourine*. New York: Harper & Row, 1983.

>Another collection of Jewish folk tales and stories drawn from the Talmud, Mishnah, and Aggadah, as well as from Jewish communities in Eastern Europe, Spain, etc.

Warshawsky, Gale Solotar. *Creative Puppetry for Jewish Kids*. Denver: A.R.E. Publishing, Inc., 1985.

>This book offers suggestions and complete instructions for making various kinds of puppets.

## *For Children*

Alda, Arlene. *Matthew and His Dad*. New York: Simon and Schuster, 1983.

>Illustrated by excellent photographs, this book describes the special relationship between a young boy and his father.

Barrett, John. *No Time for Me*. New York: Human Sciences Press, 1979.

>A child is resentful of the very hectic work schedule of a mother and father who are both lawyers. The way the matter is resolved is the central theme of this book.

Bayer, Steve and Ilene. *Mischa and Rachel*. Rockville, MD: Kar-Ben Copies, Inc., 1989.

>This book describes the process by which a Russian immigrant to Israel becomes acclimated to his new country.

Berger, Terry. *Feelings*. New York: Human Sciences Press, 1971.

>A picture book of emotions that is an excellent resource for young children.

_____. *I Have Feelings*. New York: Human Sciences Press, 1971.

>This excellent book helps young children to express and describe emotions.

Boyd, Selma, and Pauline Boyd. *The How: Making the Best of a Mistake*. New York: Human Sciences Press, 1981.

>This book deals with the aftermath of a mistake.

Cohen, Floreva. *Hanukiah for Dina*. New York: Board of Jewish Education of Greater New York, 1987.

>The author, an early childhood consultant, depicts in a loving fashion the special relationship between a young girl and her grandfather.

_____. *My Special Friend*. New York: Board of Jewish Education of Greater New York, 1986.

>This exceptional book describes a unique friendship between two children, one of whom has Down Syndrome.

Cohen, Miriam. *Will I Have a Friend?* New York: Macmillan Publishing Co., 1967.

>In clear language, this beautifully illustrated book deals with relationships among children in a nursery school.

Feinberg, Miriam. *Just Enough Room*. New York: United Synagogue of America, 1991.

>This delightful story describes hospitality on Shabbat.

Gallant, Janet. *My Brother's Bar Mitzvah*. Rockville, MD: Kar-Ben Copies, Inc., 1990.

>The celebration of a sibling's Bar Mitzvah is lovingly described.

Goldstein, Andrew. *My Very Own Jewish Home*. Rockville, MD: Kar-Ben Copies, Inc., 1987.

>Objects that identify a home as a Jewish home are described and shown in photographs.

Greene, Laura. *Help: Getting To Know About Needing and Giving*. New York: Human Sciences Press, 1981.

>Through simple, easy to understand language, the author conveys the idea that all of us need help at one time or another.

Hazan, Barbara Shook. *If It Weren't for Benjamin [I'd Always Get to Lick the Spoon]*. New York: Human Sciences Press, 1979.

>Sibling rivalry is discussed in an easy to understand manner in this excellent supplementary resource.

Hirsh, Marilyn. *Could Anything Be Worse?* New York: Holiday House, 1974.

>Retold and illustrated by Marilyn Hirsh, this rendition of a well-known folktale tells of an overcrowded house and the means taken to make it seem more spacious.

Kellogg, S. *Johnny Appleseed*. New York: Morrow Junior Books, 1988.

>A retelling of the story of the well-known individual who was responsible for the abundance of trees in America.

Krauss, Ruth. *The Carrot Seed*. New York: Harper Collins Child Book, 1945.

>A classic, this book describes the loving care given to a carrot seed by a young boy.

Marcus, Audrey Friedman, and Raymond A. Zwerin. *But This Night Is Different*. New York: Union of American Hebrew Congregations, 1981.

>In this excellent book, the things we do at the Passover Seder are described, and a regular family dinner is compared with a Passover Seder.

Reisman, Ofra, reteller and translator. *Trees Grow in Eretz Israel*. Jerusalem: World Zionist Organization, Department of Education and Culture in the Diaspora, Early Childhood Division, 1991.

>This legend tells about an old man who planted a fig tree in the Land of Israel many, many years ago.

Schwartz, Amy. *Mrs. Moskowitz and the Sabbath Candles*. Philadelphia: Jewish Publication Society of America, 1988.

> An elderly woman prepares for and celebrates Shabbat in her new apartment. A lovely story!

Scarry, Richard. *My House*. New York: Golden Press, 1976.

> A variety of houses is described in this very colorful book.

Simon, Norma. *Different Kinds of Families*. Chicago: Whitman Publishing Co., 1976.

> Families come in various forms, styles and types, and this book describes these in words and pictures.

_____. *I Was So Mad*. Chicago: Whitman Publishing Co., 1974.

> A description of what makes a person so very angry.

Syme, Deborah Shayne. *The Jewish Home Detectives*. New York: Union of American Hebrew Congregations, 1981.

> What clues can be found to determine that this is a Jewish home? The detective finds out.

Udry, Janice May. *A Tree Is Nice*. New York: Harper and Row, 1956.

> This classic book is about trees, how we benefit from them, where they grow, and how people care for them.

Watson, Jane; Robert Switzer; and J. Cotter Hirschberg. *My Body and How it Works*. Racine, WI: Western Publishing Company, 1971.

> Written in simple language, this book describes the workings of the human body.

_____. *My Friend the Doctor*. Racine, WI: Western Publishing Co., 1971.

> A description of the special role that the doctor plays in the health care of a young child.

_____. *Sometimes I Get Angry*. Racine, WI: Western Publishing Company, 1971.

> The occasional anger of young children is depicted in this book.

———. *What the Moon Brought*. Philadelphia: Jewish Publication Society, 1942.

> In simple and clear language, each of the stories in this book focuses on a family's celebration of a Jewish holiday.

Wiggers, Raymond. *Picture Guide to Tree Leaves*. New York: Franklin Watts Publishing Co., 1991.

> This is a beautiful book that contains pictures and photographs of a variety of leaves.

Zwerin, Raymond A., and Audrey Friedman Marcus. *Shabbat Can Be*. New York: UAHC Press, 1981.

> Shabbat provides opportunities for a multitude of experiences as described in this sensitively written and beautifully illustrated book.

www.ingramcontent.com/pod-product-compliance
Lightning Source LLC
Chambersburg PA
CBHW080936300426
44115CB00017B/2839